KU-002-272

CLIPS OF THE WEEK

Best Wishes,
Tom
from Andy Jacobs

All the best, Tom!
Paul [illegible]

CLIPS OF THE WEEK

Best bloopers from talkSPORT

PAUL HAWKSBEE AND ANDY JACOBS

SIMON & SCHUSTER

London · New York · Sydney · Toronto · New Delhi

A CBS COMPANY

First published in Great Britain by Simon & Schuster UK Ltd, 2013
A CBS COMPANY

1 3 5 7 9 10 8 6 4 2

Simon & Schuster UK Ltd
1st Floor
222 Gray's Inn Road
London WC1X 8HB

www.simonandschuster.co.uk

Simon & Schuster Australia, Sydney
Simon & Schuster India, New Delhi

A CIP catalogue record for this book
is available from the British Library

Photographs courtesy of talkSPORT

ISBN 978-1-47113-358-9
ebook ISBN 978-1-47113-359-6

Typeset in UK by M Rules
Printed and bound by CPI Group (UK) Ltd, Croydon, CR0 4YY

To Karen and Sue, for putting up with us for *far* too long.

CONTENTS

ACKNOWLEDGEMENTS

Paul and Andy would like to thank Dennie Morris for going above and beyond as he always does, Melissa Rudd for painstakingly transcribing all of the clips, assistant producers Tom Marshall and Carly Warren, Polly and Ugo on the decks, gaffers Liam Fisher, Bill Ridley and the man who came up with the idea for this book, Calum Macaulay – plus all of our production teams over the years, any talkSPORT colleague who's ever suggested a clip and, of course, the listeners, without whom . . .

INTRODUCTION

Had we known that *Clips of the Week* would run for more than 13 years and counting – and become something of a talkSPORT institution in the process – we might have given it a slightly less lame title.

Well, it's not very snappy, is it? We could have at least incorporated 'cock-ups', 'bloopers' or even 'gaffes' in there somewhere, plus a bit of alliteration. But in all honesty, we probably weren't even sure that the idea had legs.

And why would we? Surely the ultra-professional band of talkSPORT presenters, newsreaders and sportscasters couldn't generate enough cock-ups, bloopers or gaffes to justify a regular slot on our show every Friday afternoon at 3.30? And there was categorically no way the station's ever-growing army of articulate, erudite callers would stumble over their words or say enough dumb stuff on air to pad it out even further.

Oh yes, they could.

It's amazing to think that over the many weeks, months and years that we've compiled the clips there's been only a handful of occasions when we couldn't generate enough good ones to broadcast. And that was probably only because Alan Brazil was on holiday.

Somehow, through listening to many hours of the station's quality output (always a pleasure, never a chore as far as we're concerned), getting whispered tip-offs from producers encouraging us to 'check out what Beaky said at 7.14 this morning', and, of course, the keen ears of the talkSPORT listeners who took to the feature immediately and quickly began suggesting brilliant clips of their own, we've generally managed to offer up at least a dirty dozen.

Over the years, one or two talkSPORT bosses have questioned whether the *Clips of the Week* sent the right message to the audience and the advertisers. And it's a fair point. They are, after all, a weekly celebration of our (very) occasional foot-in-mouth moments. But we see the fact that they've endured as one of talkSPORT's many virtues. In fact, we doubt whether the clips would have survived beyond Week 1 on any other radio station.

That's because the many brilliant broadcasters who have featured in them over the years have never let their egos get in the way of good content. We hope they realise that the clips are compiled and delivered with affection and with a genuine love of the station and what makes it special: its approachability, its connection with its audience, and yes, its ability to laugh at itself.

Enough of the schmaltz, what about a few *Clips of the Week*-related FAQs? Why do we play them out at 3.30 on a Friday? Well, why not? It's a bit of a 'here comes the weekend' thing. Like bringing in games on the last day of term.

Why do *we* never feature in the *Clips*? Simple answer: I think you'll find *we* never make mistakes *(ahem . . .)*.

And, probably the most F of all the FAQs, what was the first-ever talkSPORT clip we played on air? It's something we've pondered since compiling this book and have come to the conclusion that . . . we haven't got a clue. Sorry.

We can, however, recall the first collection of clips that we unearthed and performed together. They predate our time at talkSPORT and go back to when we first met and worked together on TV's *Fantasy World Cup* with David Baddiel and Frank Skinner in 1998.

Our job then was to trawl through the ITV Sport archives, find funny footage and supply the appropriate punchlines to accompany it. We'd then present our ideas to David and Frank who'd give them the gladiatorial thumb either way – usually down.

Over the course of the series, there were a few clips that we both thought were absolute gold. Unfortunately, they didn't. We'd try sneaking them back into our clips reel for a second viewing, hoping they wouldn't notice. They always did, of course. 'We've seen this three times already – and it wasn't funny the first time. Next!' seems to ring a bell.

On the day of the final transmission, David and Frank decided that we would go onto the *Fantasy Football* set and perform this collection of clips we'd championed in front of the audience who'd just watched the show, to see if they worked as well as we claimed they would have done. And so we did.

Jack Charlton dispatching a rabbit . . . Kevin Keegan on *Disney Club* teaching Winnie the Pooh – complete with giant honey pot – to head the ball more effectively . . . sweary Wolves legend Derek Dougan . . . Bobby Robson trying to say 'Abercrombie & Fitch' . . . the bloke who'd swallowed Alan Ball . . . we played them all out. And, largely because the crowd probably took pity on a couple of amateurs, they went down a storm. Maybe that was the moment we got the bug.

So, are we saying that without Skinner and Baddiel there would be no *Clips of the Week?* Well, if they want an acknowledgement, then yes. But if they want money, no.

We hope you enjoy this collection of talkSPORT *Clips of the Week*. If you're a seasoned listener, many of the clips and their perpetrators will be well known and well loved by you. In which case, prepare to indulge in some Clip Karaoke. Because all of your favourites are here – past and present: Parry, Beaky, Quinny, Keysie, Goughie, Keith 'Mr Inadvertent Innuendo' Arthur.

But even if you've never tuned into talkSPORT in your life (are you mad . . . where have you *been?*) and are just thumbing through this book in Waterstone's chuckling at Big Al's tortured pronunciation of Greek newspaper *Eletheros Typos*, then welcome, friend. There's plenty more where that came from . . .

Paul & Andy

THE LEGEND THAT IS ALAN BRAZIL

Big Al, talkSPORT's legendary *Breakfast Show* host, played upfront for Ipswich, Spurs, Manchester United and more, as well as for his native Scotland – including a World Cup in 1982. One of the UK's best speech broadcasters, he possesses a natural ease and charm that allows him to breeze through four hours of radio every morning. During his 15 years at the station, his notable co-hosts have included Mike Parry, Graham 'Beaky' Beecroft and Ronnie Irani. These days, he's joined by a hand-picked selection of friends, including ex-Arsenal midfielder Ray Parlour, avuncular boss Neil Warnock and former Spurs and Newcastle heart-throb David Ginola. A noted *bon viveur*, whose early end to the working day allows plenty of opportunity for 'socialising', Alan's warts and all, what-you-see-is-what-you-get presenting style, has furnished us with hundreds of memorable clips over the years. No doubt he'll want to claim 50 per cent of the royalties from this book – and let's face it, he'll have a point.

***Alan Brazil reflects on the previous evening's* MTV Awards ...**

'Best dancer, best videos, who was the guy, erm, who was the guy who choreo, choreog, choreogra – who put it all together?'

***Alan on TV – here he is on* The Apprentice ...**

'It's only the first time I've seen it. He's very firm, old Sugar, isn't he, ol' Sir Alan – you're fired, you're hired, get lost!'

(I'm not sure 'You're fired, you're hired, get lost' is his catchphrase.)

Alan's back at Cheltenham, with a race we've never heard of ...

'Now the 3.20 – the big one – the Queen Mother Champion Moose.'

Chatting to the* Mirror*'s John Cross about Carlos Tevez on holiday ...

JOHN: 'He's got his music on his iPod playing, running across the beach!'

ALAN: 'You say music, it could be Rosetta Stone. He could be learning Italian – or a bit of Spanish.'

(Think, being Argentinean, he can already get by in Spanish, Al.)

A message to the Breakfast production team – when you're doing Alan's research notes, make sure you put commas in . . .

'They're almost the equivalent of a team like Villa losing young Barry Milner and Petrov. Sorry – losing Young, Barry, Milner and Petrov.'

His definitive review of the 2008 Champions League final between Manchester United and Chelsea . . .

'Moscow, crikey – what a game it was. And to end like that. John, slipping – left leg went . . . BANG!'

(Only Alan can sum up 120 minutes plus penalties in 18 words.)

Deciding not to insult FIFA President Sepp Blatter, then does it anyway . . .

'He's done it again, this tube. Sorry, I keep saying that. But Sepp Blatter – and what a numpty by the way . . .'

A unique insight into an unorthodox motivational technique . . .

'Know your players. Some need a kick up the backside – some just need an arm.'

(Not up the backside, we hope.)

Alan reporting live from the Open Golf Championship ...

'It's just gone 9.32. Don't forget, Andy Gray coming up at ten o'clock, here on the *Sports Breakfast*. 9.32. Tiger, with his ball on the left-hand side. It's 9.32, here on talkSPORT.'

(Sorry Al, we didn't quite catch the time ...)

With a fantastic link ...

('Get Back' by the Beatles playing)
'Tell you what, Billy Preston actually played with the Beatles on that one – but can Preston sneak into the play-offs and get back to the promised land?'

(We can see what you did there, Al.)

Recalling an old opponent ...

'I was trying to think of great Austrian players, and the only one I could really come up with I played against at Ipswich a long time ago – it was Franz Klammer.'

(Who could forget the way the skiing legend slalomed through defences?)

A hands across the water moment from the big man during the Finance section ...

'Tough times for Japan. Not that I care ...'

Talking to Manchester Evening News Sports Editor Peter Spencer about Wayne Rooney, Alan launches into one of his trademark lengthy questions . . .

ALAN: 'Peter, what about, you know, it's hard to get to the bottom of this because a year ago, I loved him the way he was, he led the line, he just led Man United, he was strong, you know, he was just fantastic. The punters loved his attitude, chasing back, getting tackles in, apart from scoring brilliant goals. Now all of a sudden, is it, you know, I'm trying to get to the bottom of it, what's happened? The World Cup was a disaster, was that because of off-the-field antics? All right, allegedly and all this. Or has something been bothering him for a while about United? I don't know you know, people have, footballers sometimes always think the grass is greener on the other side, they speak to Ronaldo, people like that. Or can we look even deeper? We had a call earlier talking about the problem with the Irish who sold to the Glazers. The Glazers have this huge, huge debt hanging over their heads and at the moment United's cashflow looks after that. But what if one of their other businesses is maybe not pulling its horns in, or the money that it did, so they have to pull their horns in and perhaps something's got to give? Now, is it a deeper, deeper problem than what we know about, or have we heard anything there?'

PETER SPENCER: 'Bloody hell Alan, that was a question and a half, wasn't it?'

But it's not all long questions with Alan. Here's one he posed to journalist Chris Davies …

'Chris. Wolves?'

Recalling the Champions League final with former United centre-back Henning Berg …

ALAN: 'Henning, take me back to the wonderful triumph, the wonderful year of 1999. I'm told Alex Ferguson gave a real rousing, tremendous speech just before you walked out on the pitch – can you remember that?

HENNING: 'No.'

Summing up the career of Denis Law in his own inimitable fashion …

'Sleeves down over his hands – aggressive. You know, hung in the air – BOOM! Exploded – BANG! Bent double – BOOF!'

With news of the England captaincy …

'Rio Ferdinand has reclaimed the captain's armbag from Stevie Gerrard.'

With some surprise news on Bolton chairman Phil Gartside …

'I did hear them talking about Phil Gartside coming out.'

Looking ahead to the second FA Cup semi-final . . .

'It's gonna be an absolute cracker. Chelsea have to play Sunday night, they don't want to, but the FA won't bulge.'

Discussing a great Pakistani bowler with co-host Ronnie Irani . . .

RONNIE: 'When it comes to skill and performance, there's probably no better bowler the world has seen than Wasim Akram.'

ALAN: 'Brian Lara said that as well, he said: "Azim Wazi – the most outstanding bowler I've ever faced."'

(One for the Sooty fans, there. 'Azim Wazi, let's get, er . . . Bazi.')

Introducing a special guest . . .

'He'll soon be treading the boards with the West End production of *Fences* – delighted to welcome Lenny Henry. Morning, Henry!'

(Bit public school that, Al.)

On American politics . . .

'Very interested in this story – Sir Burruck Obama back in for another term . . .'

With an unfortunate turn of phrase that sends a shiver down your spine . . .

'Plenty of action in the Football League tonight; let's have a quickie with the Moose.'

Apparently not happy that tramps are getting verbally abused . . .

'The clubs should be docked points if they can't control their supporters. It's not nice when you know you suffer hobo-phobic chants.'

Former Premier League manager Neil Warnock speaks for the nation, as Alan takes us on a geographical tour of Renfrewshire ahead of Rangers v St Mirren . . .

ALAN: 'I was going to say it's a Glasgow derby but St Mirren are up in Paisley now aren't they? I say now, they've always been out there. In fact, that is probably closer to Ibrox than Parkhead, I think. Well, Love Street used to be right up from Glasgow Airport, so it was nothing – just a flick from Ibrox to Love Street. I don't know where St Mirren Park is now. Someone will text or email me . . . Oh, six miles, is it? So that would be . . . would that be . . . I was going to say that would be closer. I don't know. Parkhead's not that far from Ibrox . . .'

NEIL: 'Listen, I'm not really bothered, Alan. Can we move on?'

At the Cheltenham Festival, crossing to reporter Rupert Bell . . .

'Let's go back out to the course, it looks an absolute picture, maybe a little bit of frost early on that's departed now. Here's talkSPORT's Rupert Bear.'

With a bizarre combined cricket score and time check . . .

'OK, Australia, 201 for eight o'clock. How does that affect the sporting odds?'

(It'll be quite dark by then, so we imagine they'll lengthen, Al.)

There'd been talk of Becks going as far as Australia, but according to Alan he was considering moving even further away . . .

'Good morning. David Beckham is set to leave the galaxy next month.'

Alan Brazil has a rare gift . . .

'We're just reminiscing about the forthcoming Ryder Cup and the St Leger.'

(He's the only man who can reminisce about something that hasn't happened yet.)

With a winning turn of phrase . . .

'It's a bit like a kettle calling another kettle black.'

And another …

'United started like a train on fire.'

And surely not another …

'Darren Lewis has really put the cat amongst the bags …'

Well done to Al on winning talkSPORT employee of the month, awarded for being the ultimate company man …

RONNIE: 'Listening to talkSPORT on the iPhone is brilliant. I did it over in China, Al. We've got to get you that!'
ALAN: 'Ah, who cares!?!'

SHOCKING ON-AIR CONFESSIONS

They say honesty is the best policy, but just occasionally we'd take a little white lie now and again. These are just a few of the moments when presenters, guests and listeners should maybe have phrased it a touch better, chosen their words carefully – or simply been more economical with the truth.

Fisherman's Blues *presenter Keith Arthur proving he's not a bloke to mess with . . .*

'I apologise to followers who have signed up to follow me on twitter. I did have someone posing as me that I eliminated.'

(Eliminated? Did he use a harpoon?)

Andy Gray telling Richard Keys about his holiday . . .

'We had a long lunch with Glenn Hoddle and his wife Vanessa. It was the one poor day we had over there.'

(And we thought they were friends . . .)

Let's head over to* Extra Time *and get the very latest up to the minute news from our Indian cricket correspondent, Dileep Premachandan, on England's warm-up game . . .

MIKE GRAHAM: 'England closed yesterday on 369 for nine. It's moved on from then, hasn't it?
DILEEP: 'Yes it has – although I haven't been following it this morning because I've been on my way to a meeting.'

(Oh, sorry to bother you.)

A caller to George Galloway . . .

GEORGE: 'Here's Francis in Swindon.'
CALLER: 'Sorry George, I haven't got my teeth in.'

Ronnie Irani surprised us all with this one . . .

ALAN: 'What are you up to today?'
RONNIE: 'I've got to go over to Gestingthorpe to see an old boyfriend of mine.'

Jonny Gould on* Extra Time *. . .

'What an amazing year. Can you remember a better 2012 for British sport? Because I can't!'

(Who can?)

***PFA Chairman Clarke Carlisle on the* Sports Breakfast ...**

ALAN BRAZIL: 'Did you see Patrice Evra after the game last night, Clarke? Someone threw an imitation arm onto the pitch and he's got a picture in the paper biting it. And I just thought, "No, think please before you do things like that."'

CLARKE: 'Sorry I didn't see that, Alan. I was watching *Broadchurch*.'

Mike Parry with an anecdote ...

'What happened was, at about five o'clock the next morning I suddenly woke up, rolled over and kissed the person on the head who was next to me. But it wasn't the girl – it was my mate! Of course he was horrified, he leapt up and threw a punch at me and I had to explain I thought he was a woman! It was all a terrible mistake. Anyway, it only lasted seconds, it was a misunderstanding and I assure you I have no heterosexual tendencies – even if I did, I don't suppose it would matter these days.'

THERE'S NO ANSWER TO THAT

A select handful of conversation stoppers – not always ideal on live radio!

Ronnie Irani giving a mention to an old team-mate . . .

'I've got to give out a quick shout as well to Warren Hegg, ex-Lancashire and England wicket-keeper. He's on his way to hospital where his missus's baby's on the way. Can't believe it! Baby on the way? What's he been up to?'

(Well Ronnie, when a man and a woman love each other very much . . .)

Mike Parry speaks to boxing gold medallist, James DeGale . . .

'James, what happens when a fighter bites you in the ring?'

Ronnie recalling – and indeed re-titling – an old classic TV sitcom . . .

RONNIE: 'Ain't Half Hot Man? What about that one?'
ALAN: 'What?'
RONNIE: 'Ain't Half Hot – *Man?*'

ANIMAL CRACKERS

Sick as a parrot . . . not counting any chickens . . . went down like a dying swan . . . The language of football is littered with references to the animal kingdom. Making a cameo appearance in our menagerie is presenter Mark Saggers. A highly accomplished and experienced TV and radio performer, 'Saggers' has the unusual distinction of having a surname as a nickname. After many years of being shackled by the conventions of his former employer, Mark has revelled in the freedom of working for talkSPORT. Opinionated and – occasionally – a bit shouty, his passion for engaging with the listeners has seen him pop up quite frequently in *Clips of the Week*.

Mark Saggers during Euro 2012, describing the stadium in Kiev . . .

'They look actually, funnily enough, like octopus testic-, sorry *tentacles*.

(Good recovery, Saggers . . .)

Micky Quinn, getting annoyed . . .

'The badge kissing really gets up my goat. It really does.'

We knew Mike Parry was from Chester, but we didn't know exactly what part – until now ...

'A friend of mine's sister used to look after elephants at Chester Zoo – where I was brought up.'

Ronnie Irani and Alan Brazil talk turkey ...

RONNIE: 'What kind of bird do you go for at Christmas, Al? Will you go for a black feathered one or what?'

ALAN: 'Always turkey.'

RONNIE: 'Yeah, but what *kind* of turkey? Is it black feathered?'

ALAN: 'I've no idea! One that goes bw-aaaark!'

Ronnie ahead of England v France ...

'The French have top, top players. We just hope England can defend like bisons.'

Mike Parry on canine companions ...

'We'd like to hear from you about your relationship with your dog. I think everybody would agree with me that animals are expandable.'

Alan Brazil, chatting to the National Trust's Mike Ingram …

MIKE: 'It's beautiful out there, it's like spring has come to Canary Wharf – fantastic.'
ALAN: 'Yesterday afternoon was like that. I was over in Greenwich, it was beautiful.'
MIKE: 'The daffodils are out, the squirrels are scurrying around with little acorns …'
ALAN: 'Squirrels? Shoot them!!!'

(Nice audition for the Springwatch presenter's gig, Al …)

Alan again, with news of a shock signing at the Stadium of Light …

'The headlines making the back pages this morning: *Daily Mail* – "Sunderland close in on an eel."'

(Would certainly be difficult to hold on to at corners.)

THANK YOU, CALLER . . .

The talkSPORT listeners. Bless them. Where would we be without them? Talking to ourselves, basically. We'd also be lacking a vital ingredient of the station's success – *and* we'd be a chapter light in this book. Those brave souls who choose to interact with the presenters by picking up the phone or sending an email, text, tweet or fax (remember faxes?) are the lifeblood of many a programme and, consequently, a rich source of material on a Friday afternoon. Why do they make so many appearances? Nerves undoubtedly play a part, as does passion, frustration and downright anger. Long may they prosper. Now, who's that on Line 4 . . .?

A caller to Duncan Barkes on the* Overnight *show . . .

DUNCAN: 'Joe is in Enfield – Joe you're on the air.'
CALLER: 'My toaster's just gone.'
DUNCAN: 'Sorry?'
CALLER: 'I put my toaster on and it's just popped up.'

(Thanks for sharing . . .)

A Stoke City fan on his failing manager . . .

'In terms of what Tony Pulis has done, I sort of sit on the fence with "Should he go, or should he go?"'

(Not much of a fence, is it?)

Before the world's most expensive player joined Real Madrid . . .

'Gareth Bale's got to leave Spurs. He wants to go to the next level. Wouldn't it be great to see a British player win the *D'Alon Bore*.'

(Not to be confused with the prestigious Ballon d'Or, this alternative award is given to the most boring person in D'Alon.)

A confused, long-time Toon Army foot soldier . . .

'I'm a Newcastle supporter, about sixty years old now. I remember the days of Trevor Macdonald.'

Alan welcoming one of* Breakfast*'s regular callers . . .

ALAN: 'Good morning. How are you, Sid?'
SID: 'Morning guys, how are you doing?'
ALAN: 'We're all right. What did you want to say, Sid?'
SID: 'Well, I've resisted the temptation to call in, guys . . .'

(Er, no you haven't.)

Discussing veterans bringing through the kids …

'When they do play, they cover every blade of grass, put every tackle in, and they give the youngsters so much encouragement that it gives them that impotence.'

On that old chestnut of Celtic and Rangers joining the Premier League …

'If they do say they want the two Scottish teams in there, then you're going to open up this big can of fish.'

A bit of confusion during* Breakfast *…

ALAN: 'Let's go to Bill on the line down in Canterbury. Bill, good morning.'
CALLER: 'Are you talking to me, Al?'
ALAN: 'Oh, it's Dave – sorry Dave, excuse me.'
CALLER: 'Well, Bill is my dad's name …'

(What's that got to do with anything?)

Praising one of England's most enduring midfielders …

'There's only one word for Lampard these days – pure class.'

Stan Collymore . . .

STAN: 'James is a Liverpool fan in Hitchin. (*Starts singing*) "How far to Hitchin, it's Hitchin I'm missin'!" . . . It's an old song, that is! James, good evening.'

CALLER: 'Er, it's Jamie.'

STAN: 'Sorry, Jamie. How are you, pal?'

CALLER: 'And I'm in Letchworth, by the way.'

A *caller* to Breakfast . . .

ALAN: 'Mark's a Forest fan – welcome to talkSPORT.'

CALLER: 'Hi, just a quick one – I've not been listening to the show all morning.'

(Thanks for your support, Mark.)

A call to *arms from an angry fan* . . .

'We want people who are going to fight for our club! We don't want missionaries here!'

A *rare call on the subject of ping-pong* . . .

'There's no point funding table tennis because there's more table tennis tables in China than there are people.'

Genesis bassist Mike Rutherford was a guest on the* Ian Collins Show*, and took a call from his number one fan ...

CALLER: 'Hi Mike. I've seen you several times. Hamburg, Manchester and Birmingham.'

MIKE: 'That's good.'

CALLER: 'That was in the Seventies when Phil Collins was on the drums.'

MIKE: 'Right.'

CALLER: 'The question I'd like to ask you is: How did you come up with "Solsbury Hill"? That was a brilliant, brilliant – one of the best songs I've ever heard.'

MIKE: 'Right, well unfortunately that wasn't me, that was a song by Peter Gabriel.'

CALLER: 'It was Peter, yeah, but weren't you involved in that?'

MIKE: 'No, that was the first solo album he did after leaving Genesis. But I agree, I think it's a great song.'

CALLER: 'I've seen Genesis live several times. They are one of the greatest sounding bands I have ever heard in my life ... What do you think of Supertramp?'

A caller to Mike Graham on the falling standards in education . . .

'The problem is they're five years behind all the other kids. We're bringing up generation after generation of sub-lut, sub-lat, er . . . sub-lit youths.'

Keith Arthur gets a call on* Fisherman's Blues *. . .

KEITH: 'Hi, Chris.'
CALLER: 'Hello there. Sorry to bother you.'

(It's a phone-in, mate – that's the general idea.)

An unusual call to George Galloway . . .

'I didn't come into this conversation with a pooey botty. And Kenneth Clarke didn't come to it with a pooey botty. And I don't really see what . . . what . . . Oh, I can't be bothered anymore. Bye.'

(Hopefully gone to clean himself up.)

THE BEST OF *FISHERMAN'S BLUES* . . .

The longest running fishing show on UK radio, anchored for many years by the brilliant Keith Arthur, now expertly steered by his able deputy Nigel Botherway, and still going strong each Saturday and Sunday morning from 6am. A programme so good it transcends its subject matter; you don't have to like fishing to like *Fisherman's Blues*. Regular contributors include legends of the angling fraternity such as John from Enderby and Crispy Duck (honestly, that's his name), plus the occasional drunk just home from a club wanting some advice on buying a rod, which, after eight pints, suddenly seems like a good idea. Whether expert or novice, everyone's treated with the same enthusiasm, knowledge and love for the sport. Here's just a few tales from the riverbank . . .

Host Nigel Botherway with news of a new product . . .

'In the Thames, a fish finder is fantastic for picking up the bottom feeders – but it's not that good for finding fish.'

(Well, change its name, then!)

Host Keith Arthur taking a call . . .

CALLER: 'Morning Keith. I've been fishing with a club for quite a few years now.'

(Try using a rod, mate, not bludgeoning the fish to death!)

Nigel chatting to a caller . . .

NIGEL: 'I bet that part of the riverbank was packed.'
CALLER: 'No, it was actually very quiet.'
Nigel: 'Oh, that's interesting . . .'
CALLER: 'I think it was due to Ramadan being on. And Fish-o-mania.'
NIGEL: 'Of course, Fish-o-mania.'

(Yeah, don't think a fishing competition is quite as important as one of the Five Pillars of Islam.)

And here's Nigel with the junior fishing results . . .

'In the Under-nines, Ryan won with six pound twelve, Tobias had three pound two – and Barney, nine ounces.'

(Nine ounces? Is that even technically a fish?)

Keith with a lovely heart-warming tale about how he caught his first-ever fish . . .

'How did I feel when I caught it? Excited, because I'd never seen one before. So I put it in the jar that I brought with me – then took it home and watched it die.'

Nigel and his sidekick's tribute to a famous Abbott & Costello routine . . .

NIGEL: 'Brilliant. I bet that was good fun. How did Hugh get on?'
CALLER: 'I think about twenty pound was the biggest I got.'
NIGEL: 'No sorry, I said Hugh.'
CALLER: 'Oh, Hugh had a couple of thirties.'

(Yes, but Hugh's on first, Nige?)

A caller to* Fisherman's Blues *with a bizarre tale . . .

'I was stalking fish in the rain. I've gone up this tree – all my clothes are strewn all over the place . . . I'm the only one on the lake, so it didn't matter. I'm trying to dry out on this nice sunny day. So I've gone up this willow tree and found a fish feeding . . .'

(In a tree? Flying fish, was it?)

Keith Arthur talking eels . . .

'The thing is, eels are so central to the whole thing because in my opinion – and it is my opinion – I like to use circumstantial evidence where it's available. Circumstantial evidence is sometimes frowned on, but its evidence is there because it's circumstantial – it's something that's happened. It's a circumstance.'

(Thanks for clearing that up, Keith.)

Here's a very excited caller to the show . . .

'Last year the bream at Kingston were in a spawning frenzy. If anyone knows when they're actually breeding, I'll drop everything to go down there, because I want to film it. I think everyone – your listeners, anglers, non-anglers – would love to watch the footage.'

(Not sure, mate. Can't see it knocking Downton or Luther out of the ratings.)

A caller to Keith who spotted a strange fish . . .

'I said to my wife, "Come and look at this." She said to me, "What is it?" I said, "Well, it's the shape of a bream, and the mouth and the lips on it are like Mick Jagger!"'

(As Alan might say: 'Come on! Let's have your fish-themed Stones songs! 08717 . . .')

... AND 'CARRY ON' *FISHERMAN'S BLUES ...*

Thank God for the scatological undercurrent in fishing terminology. Without it, we would have been denied hours and hours of magnificent *double entendres*. We're amazed, to this day, that such an innocent pastime as fishing often sounds so absolutely *filthy* ...

What is it that makes fishing terminology so lewd?

'You remind me of John who I met the other week. He was on the pole and he said: "Come on, come and have a go on my pole."'

And this caller to Keith Arthur ...

'I've fished against him quite a few times in the last few years, and he's given me a couple of good hidings on the waggler ...'

Keith talking dirty to a caller ...

KEITH: 'Is it twelve foot or eleven foot?'
CALLER: 'It's twelve foot.'
KEITH: 'Ah, you're probably all right then, because with a twelve foot rod you can build a bit more power into the butt. That helps, a bit of stiffness in the butt section.'

Away from* Fisherman's Blues, *even Mike Parry and Mike Graham got in on the act . . .

MIKE G: 'Imagine if you put your rod in the water and the fish didn't find it in any way allured, at all.'
MIKE P: 'You don't put your rod in the water, Mike.'
MIKE G: 'Don't you?'
MIKE P: 'No, what dangles into the water is your tackle.'

Keith on extreme weather . . .

'Mini-tornadoes happen quite regularly this time of year. You have to be very unlucky to actually be underneath one, but a chap who was talking to me said he had to actually lay down and hold on to his tackle to stop it being lifted up.'

Keith says goodbye to a caller . . .

'Good to hear from you, Willie – keep it up!'

And here's Keith living up to his reputation as talkSPORT's King of Innuendo . . .

'Stop it! Something just grabbed hold of me control box!'

And . . .

'Let me just enter into the inner sanctum of my trouser pocket . . .'

And finally, this caller . . .

'I've just been given a three-metre whip.'

(Dirty boy.)

CONFUSED? DON'T WORRY, SO ARE THEY

Just occasionally during talkSPORT's 24/7 quality output, it's to be expected that our presenters and pundits will get a touch bewildered and befuddled. Try to get your head around some of these. We're still struggling . . .

George Galloway with a request . . .

'It's a cracking show tonight. Join in, especially if you're a first-time caller – or someone who hasn't been on before.'

Journalist Chris Davies on* Breakfast *. . .

'It's wrong to expect a footballer in this day and age to have virtually no skeleton of any type, in any puzzle.'

Alan Brazil . . .

'I've got a friend – family really. My daughter's husband's sister's . . . husband.'

(Think that's second daughter-in-law twice removed . . . or something?)

Mark Saggers looking ahead to England v France in the Six Nations rugby . . .

'Could be one of those games – it could be very close, or it could actually not be close at all.'

(Well, that's cleared that one up.)

Ray Stubbs previewing the US Open . . .

'I'm delighted to say that golf correspondent Bob Bubka joins us from Merion in Pennsylvania. Bob, good evening, good morning I should say – or good afternoon . . . what time is it?'

Jason Cundy catching up with co-host Darren Gough . . .

JASON: 'You're looking well, Goughie. You been down the gym? Been on the sunbed?'
DARREN: 'Er, bit of both. No sunbed, though.'

Late, great talkSPORT presenter Mike Dickin re-enacted Abbott & Costello's 'Who's On 1st?' as he welcomed a caller . . .

MIKE: 'Derek's on The Wirral, away you go Derek.'
DEREK: 'Hello.'
MIKE: 'Hi, Derek.'
DEREK: 'Hi, Derek, hi.'
MIKE: 'No no, I'm Derek. No, you're Derek, I'm Mike. You've got me confused now.'
DEREK: 'No, it's just, err Derek, it's just to let you know . . .'
MIKE: 'No, I'm not Derek, you're Derek, I'm Mike.'
DEREK: 'You're Mike, okay.'
MIKE: 'Right, yeah.'

PURE CLASS

Despite the station's name, now and again we do venture away from the sporting arena to dabble in the arts, discuss pop culture and tackle weightier topics. Okay, so it's not quite *The South Bank Show* or *Newsnight* – but, then again, could *they* get 20 minutes out of England's left-sided problem? We think not . . .

Let's raise the tone, as Ronnie Irani discusses great literature . . .

'What about John Steinbeck's *Of Mice And Me?*'

And here's the equally well read Mike Parry . . .

'Puck is the name of the guy in the Rudyard Kipling book in 1906. Well, you've heard of Puck the Magic Dragon, haven't you?'

(No.)

Alan Brazil talking opera with Sven-Goran Eriksson's agent, Athole Still . . .

ALAN: 'Your favourite opera is what, Athole?'
ATHOLE: 'I'd have to say *La Boheme*, Alan. It's beautiful.'
ALAN: '*La Boheme*. Am I right to say that was *Miss Saigon* on the stage?'
ATHOLE: 'No.'

Mike Parry with an upmarket competition . . .

CALLER: 'I'll take a stab and say Bordeaux, Mike.'
MIKE: 'Bordeaux. As in the tapestry, yeah?'
CALLER: 'Yeah.'

Weekend Breakfast *presenter Micky Quinn sets up the listeners' call topic of the morning . . .*

'And off the back of Saggers's man-bag and our producer Skaggsy taking his Ugg boots back to the shop after getting abuse from his mates, we want to know – what's your biggest fashion *fox pazz*?'

Alan chatting to studio guest, actor Ray Winstone . . .

ALAN: 'I need to ask you about your next film, *Noah's Ark*. It's not out yet, is it?'
RAY: 'No, it'll be out in about eighteen months.'
ALAN: 'Give us a clue, what it's about?'
RAY: 'Noah's Ark.'

Mike comes over all philosophical as he chats to Alan Brazil ...

MIKE: 'I think your prejudices overcome you sometimes, Al. Don't you know that the world is a great big onion? And everyone in that onion has to work together? Don't you realise that, Al?'

ALAN: 'No.'

This is Steve Berry on the Overnight show ...

STEVE: 'Do you remember we had this thing called the English Civil War? Are you familiar with it – the royalists and the parliamentarians?'

CALLER: 'I've read about it, but I'm way too young to probably remember that.'

(True, unless you're 370 years old ...)

And Mike Parry again, this time with an attack on co-host Mike Graham ...

'I've often regarded you as a cultural pygmy – which you are. Culturally, you are a pygmy of enormous proportions.'

Alan Brazil, discussing Morgan Freeman movies with Ronnie Irani and the Moose . . .

MOOSE: 'Of course, he has won Academy Awards for things like *Robin Hood, Million Dollar Baby, Invictus* . . .'
ALAN: 'Sheepshank!'
RONNIE: 'Oh, *Shawshank Redemption.*'
MOOSE: '*Shawshank Redemption* . . .'
ALAN: 'Sheepshank!'

(Yeah, the Sheepshank Redemption. That's the one where the former Ipswich chairman escapes Portman Road through a Raquel Welch poster.)

Mikes Parry and Graham on a famous celebrity couple . . .

MIKE G: 'I introduced my eldest daughter to Coldplay when nobody had heard of them.'
MIKE P: 'Coldplay?'
MIKE G: 'You heard of them?'
MIKE P: 'Chris Martin?'
MIKE G: 'That's right. He's married to erm . . .'
MIKE P: 'Gwyneth Cointreau.'

We're all familiar with the famous biblical quote: "Physician, heal thyself." All, it seems, apart from Mike Parry. Here's Mike Graham asking for help to keep his co-host on the wagon . . .

MIKE G: 'Anybody in Britain, at any point – whether you're on a train, or in a bar, anywhere – if they see you having a drink, I want them to let me know.'

MIKE P: 'Eh? Cure thyself surgeon!'

What was that film called with Bill Murray and Scarlett Johansson? You know, the one set in a hotel in Japan? Don't worry, Alan Brazil will know . . .

'Has he got a point? Chelsea fans probably feel he has. Mind you, he'll probably say it was lost in transfusion.'

(Lost in Transfusion, that it! Cheers, Al.)

Micky Quinn and Ray Stubbs on the great explorers . . .

QUINNY: 'Christopher Columbus first discovered the world was round. You like that Ray? I've delved into the anals of history.'

RAY: 'Sorry?'

FOOD FOR THOUGHT

The pre-match meal. For Blackburn's Alan Shearer, it was chicken and beans; for legendary England goalkeeper Gordon Banks, 'a large steak with peas and both boiled and roast potatoes, followed by a large bowl of rice pudding'. (Seriously, look it up.) For the fans, the options are either a salmonella burger from a stall outside the ground, or take out a second mortgage for a tepid watery pie inside the stadium. What we're trying to say is, food and sport – they kind of go together, don't they? Well, for the sake of the next selection of culinary clips they do anyway …

Here's Scotland's Cultural Attaché to China, Alan Brazil …

'We're heading to Beijing. Couldn't you just kill for a spring roll right now?'

Mark Saggers on* Kick Off*, clearly feeling a bit peckish …

'There will be a few of those who say Michael Appleton went from Portsmouth to Blackpool, and he's now gone to Blackburn … it's been a case of footballing korma.'

(Probably a chicken korma, Mark, as it's Venkys.)

A caller to Breakfast ...

'I'd be surprised if Alex Oxtail-Chamberlain isn't playing.'

This is Mark Saggers and football expert Gab Marcotti overusing the phrase 'chicken resources' ...

MARK: 'They are big players. These guys own most of the chicken resources in India.'
GAB: 'Who owns most of the chicken resources in the UK?'
MARK: 'The Venkys!'
GAB: 'No, in the UK.'
MARK: 'Oh, I don't know, haven't got a clue.'
GAB: 'That's what I mean – so is it a big deal?'
MARK: 'Yes, it's a massive deal.'
GAB: 'I'm sure they're wealthy but ...'
MARK: 'I'll tell you one thing, there's a consortium of fourteen different guys who own a lot of the chicken resources over here. They're doing okay – chicken is a big thing as you can imagine. And the Venkys are really big in chicken.'

(And, indeed, chicken resources.)

Alan Brazil gets Mao Tse-tung spinning in his grave, then suffers a bit of culinary confusion during the* Breakfast's *'On This Day' feature . . .

'Now the People's Republic of China proclaimed Maxi Chung (sic) as its Chairman on this day in 1949. I tell you what, what a result that is – I love a ruby!'

Richard Keys and Andy Gray discuss domestic matters . . .

RICHARD: 'How was the beef stew?'

ANDY: 'Let me tell you, Richard. I got home last night and the beef stew was amazing. I have to congratulate my missus. She was very worried about it, we had six of the family round with us last night – and the beef stew was presented and I have to say . . . it was lamb, actually – lamb stew.

(Can't have been that good if you couldn't even tell what the meat was, Andy!)

A worrying caller to the* Overnight *show . . .

CALLER: 'I'd have no problem eating humans.'

MIKE GRAHAM: 'Humans?'

CALLER: 'I'm serious – I think it's an absolute waste . . .'

MIKE: 'But that'd make you a cannibal!?'

CALLER: 'I don't care what it would make me. It would make me a human being wanting to survive and beat the credit crunch.'

(No, it would make you a cannibal.)

Mike Parry having a night out down the boozer ...

'I enjoy a packet of peanuts with a pint of shandy, but I want to know what the peanuts are first. People think I'm mad. I go into a pub and they say: "Hi, what can I get you, Sir?" and I say, "First of all, what kind of penis do you sell?"'

... and he'd been wondering why his diet wasn't working ...

'If you'd said to me you had a salad, and part of the salad is sardines and some lettuce and, I don't know, a bit of a pork pie ...'

(Nice slimming pork pie ...)

LET'S JOIN YOUR COMMENTATOR . . .

Matterface, McKenna and Adderley. Not a firm of solicitors or even a Seventies supergroup, just three of the fine broadcasters who call games for talkSPORT. Their job is to paint pictures with words, but – as the next selection illustrates – they do very occasionally drip emulsion onto the shag pile . . .

Sam Matterface is clearly shorter than he looks . . .

'I bumped into Per Mertesacker in the tunnel at Arsenal on Wednesday night after that Swansea game. He is *massive*. Six foot, six inches – he's almost double my size.'

We knew things weren't going particularly well at Liverpool at the time, but we didn't realise they were this bad . . .

'You're listening to Liverpool nil, talkSPORT nil.'

Sam at Old Trafford . . .

'Here's Robin van Persie down the left-hand side . . . Gerrard tries to nip in and manages to just get one of his right legs round the back of Van Persie . . .'

And Sam suddenly thinking he's the Queen ...

'Twenty-five minutes into the second half. We're going to take a corner on this nearside.'

This is Andrew McKenna with breaking news ...

'Tonight's League Two game between Rotherham and Morecambe will have to pass a piss inspection.'

(It might burn a small area of grass, but we're sure the game will go ahead.)

And we love it when our match reporters give it the big sell, don't you?

'After a postponement and a nil-nil draw, this least attractive of third round draws will be decided on this cold dark evening in the least attractive of conditions.'

Sam Matterface at the end of Sunderland v Spurs ...

'Bardsley wants to get it forward, it's hoisted to the edge of the box, the referee puts the ball to his lips – and the full-time whistle blows at the Stadium of Light!'

Graham Beecroft previewing Blackpool v Spurs . . .

'DJ Campbell is the leading scorer for Blackpool. Charlie Adam is up there as well with him, scoring plenty of goals – but he's the heart-throb of the midfield.'

(Charlie Adam. Phwoarr . . .)

Beeky again, during the same match . . .

'It looks as though it's going to be a dramatic win here for Blackpool, although Spurs, as you might imagine, are still going at it hammer and tongues.'

WHERE IN THE WORLD?

Time to rack up the air miles and take a global jaunt with the presenters and punters who, on this evidence, probably failed GCSE Geography . . .

Alan Brazil worried about travelling around South Africa for the World Cup . . .

'I wouldn't want to be over there, wandering about lost, trying to find my way back to Jo'burg or to Cape Town. Or Dublin.'

(Er, we think he means Durban . . .)

This is the presenter of talkSPORT's Scottish phone-in, Arthur Albiston, chatting to a caller . . .

CALLER: 'I was wondering about Craig Burley's selection of the Scotland squad.'

ALBISTON: 'Yep.'

CALLER: 'I just don't know why, for at least three seasons, he's been ignoring Antti Niemi.'

ALBISTON: 'Antti Niemi?'

CALLER: 'Aye. I don't know why he doesn't get a game.'

ALBISTON: 'For Scotland?'

CALLER: 'Aye.'

ALBISTON: 'But he's from Finland.'

CALLER: 'He's what?'

ALBISTON: 'He's Finnish?'
CALLER: 'He's no' finished, he's only twenty-eight!'
ALBISTON: 'No, not finished, he's from Finland!'
CALLER: 'What do you mean?'
ALBISTON: 'That's where he's . . . His nationality is Finnish. He's from Finland.'
CALLER: 'He's not Scottish?'
ALBISTON: 'No.'
CALLER: 'Oh. I thought he was Scottish.'

And a caller to Mark Saggers:

MARK: 'Nas is a Liverpool fan from Turkey. Nas, good evening.'
NAS: 'I'm calling from Purley actually, South London.'
MARK: 'Oh, Purley!'

(So not that near to Turkey, then.)

Drive *presenter Darren Gough chatting to a guest . . .*

GOUGHIE: 'Alexandra, where are you from?'
ALEXANDRA: 'I'm from Finland.'
GOUGHIE: 'Finland, eh? Do you speak Finnish?'

Mike Parry looks ahead to the 2010 World Cup and discovers a new country . . .

'I know there are some really poor countries, like Bolaros.'

Alan Brazil greets phone guest and former Manchester United defender Henning Berg . . .

'Good morning, Henning! Henning, where are we talking to you from?'

(Our guess would be the talkSPORT studio.)

Ronnie Irani reads Alan a listener's nomination for the best-ever movie soundtrack . . .

RONNIE: 'Guys, just tuned in, surely top film tune 2001 – "Betty Purely."'
ALAN: 'Eh?'
RONNIE: 'There you go – top film tune in 2001 – "Betty Purely."'
ALAN: 'Eh? You're not reading it right.'
RONNIE: 'I am!'
ALAN: 'You're not. Give it to me . . . it's Betty in Purley!!'

And it wasn't the first time he'd done it . . .

RONNIE: 'Got a great text here from Simon, saying I'm in Rotterdam at my Ma and Pa's house listening to your fantastic show . . .'
ALAN: 'No, really? Rotterdam?
RONNIE: 'Is there any chance you can give a discreet mention to Phillip and Dorothy in Rotter– oh no, *Rotherham.*'

Mike Parry with some local knowledge . . .

'Lancashire is the home of the Lancashire Hot Pot, the home of roast beef and Yorkshire pudding . . .'

Alan with transfer news . . .

'George Friend, Exeter to Wolves – undisclosed fee. Peter Gulacsi, to a team in Hungaria.'

Mike Parry, out at the 2010 World Cup, with news of a famous South African local . . .

'It is a poetic country, this. You've got to remember that Rudyard Kipling was born not two and a half thousand miles from here actually.'

(Bet he's something of a local hero.)

A caller to Duncan Barkes on the Overnight show discussing how badly we handle the snow in the UK . . .

CALLER: 'You look at the other countries, they manage all the time – why don't we?'
DUNCAN: 'Which countries?'
CALLER: 'I don't know, Russia, America – they all deal with the snow. Mexico . . .'

(Mexico?!)

Mike Parry reminiscing about a trip to an iconic cricket ground down under . . .

'I've been to the WACA, believe it or not. I went there before I went swimming with monkeys.'

(Even David Attenborough hasn't done that.)

Mike again, with some surprise cricket news . . .

'Let's find out what has happened in the first Twenty20 – Austria versus England.'

(How could we forget 'The Blue Danube' by Andrew Strauss?)

Jason Cundy and Micky Quinn on the* Weekend Sports Breakfast *. . .

JASON: 'I was in Jamaica on holiday playing beach volleyball and one of the guys said his name was Oscar. Turns out it was Oscar De La Hoya!'

QUINNY: 'Ugh, a man playing beach volleyball with a pair of those budgie jugglers on. No thank you!'

(Well, if you can't smuggle 'em, juggle 'em . . .)

Alan Brazil on the popularity of the Premier League in the Far East . . .

'In Asia, it's amazing how many people watch. When I used to commentate for ESPN, there were 600 people every week who used to watch it.'

(Clearly not as popular then, as it is now.)

It was good of Niall Hickman of the* Daily Express *to chat to Andy Goldstein and Jason Cundy despite being overseas . . .

HICKMAN: 'I'm looking at the Empire State Building at the moment, guys.'
CUNDY: 'Really? Where are you?'

(Er, Reykjavik?)

OH DEAR, WHAT CAN THE MATTER BE?

Lavatorial humour – it's not clever and it's not funny. Okay, it can be funny. We'd like to say we're above it, but we'd be lying . . .

High drama at talkSPORT! Let's join Mark Saggers with the breaking news . . .

'This is the most bizarre situation we've been in for some time. Dear old Quinny has dashed out to the loo and he's rung our producer to say he can't get back out through the door! He's locked himself in there – he's stuck in the loo! You couldn't make it up. I don't know what we're going to do about that. Can we not just smash the door down or something?'

A rather personal question from Alan . . .

'Tommy, as a manager, how important is it that you can have a good number two?'

Stan Collymore watching Chelsea v QPR . . .

'The pitch really is starting to cut up. Lots of brown patches, lots of skidmarks . . .'

(A nightmare for the kit man.)

Mike Parry on the subject of charging for the loos on Ryanair ...

ALAN: 'Just don't have your usual three bottles of wine on the plane and you don't have to go to the loo, do you!?!'

MIKE: 'Al, it's not as simple as that. Suppose the guy next to you – remember these planes go to foreign climes – has got a dickie tummy because he's got the old Mozzarella's Curse?'

North-east correspondent Graham Courtney has shock news about one of the Stoke strikers ...

'Kenwyne Jones has been far from regular in the past two or three months.'

(He should try All Bran.)

Jason Cundy explaining why he arrived late to the studio ...

'Fifty-five minutes it's taken me to get from Covent Garden on the tube. Fifty-five minutes! I should have just dumped in a cab, to be honest.'

Mick Dennis of the Daily Express, clearly in a bit of discomfort ...

'In the same way our complaints about the election were seen as sore grapes ...'

(We find Preparation H works for us.)

INSIDE THE MIND OF MIKE 'PORKY' PARRY

Self-confessed member of 'Her Majesty's gutter press', one time tabloid hack, former talkSPORT controller and *Breakfast* show co-host, Mike has a no-nonsense style that sometimes strays into simple nonsense. The listeners love Mike's espousal of ludicrous theories backed up with his unshakeable belief in his ideas, however daft the hypothesis. Who could forget racehorses with wing mirrors, goal frames the width of the pitch, or his contention that someday soon a man will run the 100 metres in one second? A lovable force of nature, over the years Mike's crackpot theories and winning turn of phrase have provided us with as much material as anyone. Let's enter the world of a truly original thinker . . .

Mike's never afraid to ask the big questions . . .

'Who is the most famous ventriloquist dummy in Britain now? It's still Sooty, isn't it?'

Talking snooker . . .

'Snooker is very different. Snooker is played in the dark.'

(That wouldn't be great for the spectators.)

Discussing Shaolin monks ...

'You can't qualify and call yourself a Shaolin monk unless you pass the final test – which is that you can stick your right foot in your mouth.'

Arguing about football with a listener ...

MIKE: 'You've ignored one very important point, and that is that on his day Michael Owen is one of the world's great strikers.'

CALLER: 'Yeah, on his day, but he's not fit!'

MIKE: 'Well, he's not at the moment, but I'm not a paediatrician ...'

With a competition ...

'We've got our five contestants ready – what you have to do is get every one right. So if you're the first contestant, you have to get all five right to get to the end and be today's winner. That's the toughest job in the world, being the first contestant in this competition.'

(Yes, toughest job in the world. That's put all of you firefighters and bomb disposal experts in your place.)

And if the Daily Star's Mike Ward can't do our TV preview one Monday, then Mike Parry would be a worthy replacement . . .

'Guess what I've been watching on satellite TV again? *What's-his-name and What's-his-name Deceased*. What's it called?'

(Randall and Hopkirk, but that's close enough.)

Actually, we're quite worried about Mike . . .

MIKE: 'I find it odd when you go into corner shops which have a machine in saying "Get Money Here."'

ANDY TOWNSEND: 'They never work anyway.'

MIKE: 'Well, even if they do I'm a bit suspicious that there's a man in there and as soon as you push your card in, he takes a note of your number and pushes it out again and takes a few quid.'

(We wouldn't lose any sleep over it, Mike.)

Making friends in Austria . . .

MIKE: 'Is this your little girl here on the bar?'

WOMAN: 'No, it's my son! It's a boy!'

With an original theory on aviation ...

'Why can't aeroplanes run on steam engines? I don't understand it at all. I can't understand why man cannot make steam engines as efficient as a petrol engine. Because we've done it with diesel – diesel is now more efficient than a petrol engine! What you laughing at?'

(Just imagine shovelling coal into the boiler at 35,000 feet.)

We all know Mike's good at maths – but what about spelling?

'Text CASH – That's C-S-H.'

Chatting about his musical aspirations with co-host Andy Townsend ...

MIKE: 'I've always wanted to play a musical instrument and I've thought about the violin.'

ANDY: 'What about the guitar or a piano? You know you could play that anywhere.'

MIKE: 'I'll tell you why – everybody plays the guitar don't they? And everybody plays the piano. And to play the piano, you've got to have a piano to play on.'

Talking about a top female athlete ...

'The greatest compliment anyone can give her is you watch her in a race and you can't pick her out. She looks just like a man.'

(We're sure she's really flattered.)

With some advice for a listener ...

'We suggest you log on to www-dot-HMRC, as in 'Her Majesty's ... RC.'

Bantering with a listener ...

'The reason they're shaking your hand, mate, is out of sympathy because they think you've got some kind of mental derangement to be walking around in a Stanley Accrington shirt.'

(Stanley Accrington? Didn't he play for Accrington Stanley in the Fifties?)

With news from what must be the Isle of Man ...

'When the mountain rescue service finds you moaning and wailing at the bottom of the valley, they just dial the number and say: "We've got a man here with three broken legs."'

Tackling religion ...

'Christianity, basically, is represented by Cliff Richard, isn't it?'

With Connie Fisher in the studio, seamlessly segueing back and forth from the Sound of Music star into the travel . . .

'We're going to go over to Gemma in a second to talk about traffic – talking of traffic . . . traffic of course, roads, roads lead to places, we've got Connie Fisher coming in the studio today to talk about her forthcoming UK tour, which stretches all the way from Croydon – the Fairfield Halls – all the way to the Marina Theatre in Lowestoft, via places like Reading and Chatham and New Brighton – the Floral Pavilion in Liverpool. Right, let's find out if the roads are going to be clear NOW – rather than when Connie goes on tour in September. Let's talk to Gemma . . .'

(Or maybe Gemma could give us a few bars of 'My Favourite Things'?)

Here's why Mike would never make a London cabbie . . .

'It looked to me like they'd just abandoned the Highway Code in Trafalgar Circus.'

. . . or a geography teacher . . .

MIKE PARRY: 'The only place in the world where German is spoken is Germany.'
MIKE GRAHAM: 'That's not true.'
MIKE P: 'It is true. Where else is it spoken?'
MIKE G: 'It's spoken in Austria.'
MIKE P: 'Austria is Germany!'

... or, indeed, a doctor ...

'Remember, the further you go up the greasy pole, once they re-grease the pole you come down again – bang! And then you get what I call broken anus syndrome when you hit the ground.'

Mikes Parry and Graham talking modern-day chivalry, with a slightly sinister turn of phrase ...

MIKE G: 'Women in 2010 will quite happily buy you a drink.'

MIKE P: 'I don't agree with you. You should say to a woman: "You're my guest, you're in my custody this weekend ... "'

(Custody? Beware the future Mrs Parry ...)

Here's the pair of them dredging up the past ...

MIKE P: 'Why do you think we are still debating to this day the disappearance of Glenn Miller?'

MIKE G: 'Eh? Glenn Miller?'

MIKE P: 'The disappearance of Glenn Miller – the famous band leader.'

MIKE G: 'I've *never* debated the disappearance of Glenn Miller. When was the last time you debated the disappearance of Glenn Miller?'

MIKE P: 'I have a conversation about it once a week.'

(There are members of the Miller family who don't discuss it that much!)

Mike's strong views on gouging in rugby …

'Why do people get punished for six months if it's an accident? You don't punish people for accidents. You'll have rugby players setting fire to each other next. That's the same sort of offence. I'm telling you, it is a horrendous, heinous offence to go round gouging a man's eye out. It's tantamount to setting fire to somebody!'

And, believe it or not, he actually took it a stage further …

MIKE: 'Gouging should carry a life ban. It's tantamount to murder.'
ANDY TOWNSEND: 'Is that a little bit too extreme?'
MIKE: 'No! It is tantamount to MURDER!'

Mike's proved himself to be something of a genius when it comes to improvising alternative song lyrics on the hoof. Who could possibly forget his reworking of this Rod Stewart classic …

'If you think I'm sexy, and you're going to love me, come on baby open wide! If you think I'm groovy, and you wanna smooch me, come on baby by my side!'

And what about this expert re-imagining of the Jacksons' hit 'Blame It On The Boogie' …

'Don't talk about the sunshine, don't talk about the daytime …'

(… don't blame it on the red wine, blame it on the boogie!)

Mike Parry, chatting with Alan about Tony Adams and the cerebral managers . . .

'The point I'm making is that deep-thinking people shouldn't think too deeply.'

Mike on the environment . . .

'The world is a living orgasm.'

It's bathtime with Mr P . . .

MIKE GRAHAM: 'You cannot have a bath instantly.'
MIKE P: 'Yes you can!'
MIKE G: 'It requires planning.'
MIKE P: 'Well, you've got to run a bit of water into the bath obviously.'
MIKE G: 'Exactly, and that takes some time.'
MIKE P: 'Not in mine – I have a very high speed bath filler.'
MIKE G: 'Have you?'
MIKE P: 'Well . . . a tap.'

Mike on his Christmas rituals . . .

'On Christmas Day, in our family you eat in the household and sing carols and you have the tree and you watch *The Snowman*. I love *The Snowman*, reduces me to tears – *(sings)* "We're flying through the air!"'

(Yes Mike, you love it so much you can't remember the words.)

Yes, no one celebrates Christmas quite like Mike …

'In the old days, I can understand why Boxing Day was such a popular day to get out. Go and have a ski on the Thames because it's frozen – or have a bonfire on the Thames. But stand well back, of course, because the bonfire will melt the ice.'

(We don't even know where to start with that one …)

With a proud boast …

'I can peel an orange without breaking the skin on it.'

(Even David Blaine can't do that.)

Here's Mike reminiscing …

'Last summer, I remember – I have a long memory – I had to meet somebody because we were going off to something somewhere …'

(The devil's in the detail …)

On the Romans …

'The Romans used to drink wine instead of water because wine was easier to manufacture than water.'

NOT-SO-WELL-KNOWN PHRASES OR SAYINGS

A collection of utterances unlikely ever to enter the vernacular, briefly starring *Kick Off* presenter and co-commentator supreme, Stan Collymore. A football icon who played at the very highest level, Stan's enthusiasm and passion for football knows no bounds and his love of the game always shines through. As he shows here, he's also able to improvise every bit as well with the English language as he did leading England's attack . . .

Andy Gray with a famous phrase . . .

'The guy's box office and he delivers. It's like that old phrase: "If you're high maintenance, then you'd better be good."'

(Remember your old Nan telling you that one?)

Stan Collymore remodelling an old phrase . . .

'They stood like statues, the Bolton back-four. All looked to put their hands up – not a cat on earth's chance!'

The Moose on Chelsea's scoring sensation, Oscar . . .

'It's an absolutely stunning goal from a twenty-year-old kid. I mean, if he carries on like this, the world is literally at his oyster.'

THE MAKING OF . . . *CLIPS OF THE WEEK*

/e are very proud of the *Clips of the Week* and there really is nothing etter than receiving a tweet or text from someone who's said they lmost crashed the car listening to the show, or the person in traffic next) them can't understand why they're laughing so much! The process of rriving at the dozen or so that make up each week's selection is pretty 1uch unchanged over the years . . .

Our producer 'Fulham Jon' collects all the clips suggested during the week...

...and passes them nto to the boffins o edit into bite-sized chunks.

Some of the clips are suggested by the talkSPORT listeners...

...others by the team, especially Andy with his famed 'prostate specials' – those clips he hears while doing something important in the wee small hours...

[illegible]
[illegible] Shrittler [illegible] RA – [illegible] had a [illegible]
[illegible] on the Roof.
Blair [illegible] Jon Scarlett.
7.14 [illegible] I used to be known as dead eyed dick
(I don't know about the dead eye bit)
18 Our old favourite the [illegible]
now got fingers
also; agreed to do a [illegible]

...which he then logs in his legendary Clips Book.

On Friday morning, our assistant producer 'The Sultan' plays us the clips. We usually start with around 25–35, aiming to end up with a quality dozen or so.

Those that make us laugh...

...make it into the Clips of the Week.

Those that don't…

…don't.

aul then writes
he intros and
hat Stuart
earce might call
he 'humourable'
ay-off lines
round the
elected clips.

. T/S CALLER OF W. TO F/BLUES...
4. ANDY GOLDSTEIN - PREPARES FOR HIS [illegible] ON GERMAN
RADIO . . . (GOOD MORGAN) BREAKFAST..
5. HIS CO-HOST GAVE US A HINT WHEN HE [illegible]
THIS COUPLE OF WEEKS BACK. (NEIN NEIN)
6. HOW'S DARREN GOUGH ON THE KINNEAR. (PRONUNCIATION) GIFFEN
7. [illegible] ON ASCOT (ASCOT-[illegible])
8. ALL [illegible] CLASSIC [illegible] (DESPERATE DEPTH)
9. ALAN [illegible] LINE-UP: CONCENTRATION SO MUCH
ON GETTING DEPTH RIGHT [illegible] CONCENTRATE ON WORD
[illegible] IT...
10. ALAN ON THE RELAY - ([illegible])
11. [illegible] IN THE NEXT HOUR [illegible]
FROM THE OPPOSITION.
12. ALAN REFLECTING ON [illegible] INTERVIEW (FROM BEN [illegible])

Trouble is, his
handwriting's
appalling.
So...

...he puts them in order and types them up..

...so Polly on the decks can understand them and press the right button at the right moment.

t 330pm we're
ive to the nation
nd ready to
esent the Clips
f the Week.

Some of the
talkSPORT
staff wander
into the studio
to listen...

...those hard at work tune-in at their desks.

Ten minutes later, it's all over. Paul asks the listeners to send in their clips for the following week - and the whole process starts again...

Boxer Audley Harrison on the noble art …

‘Boxing is a tough slog. People want to get educated, they don’t just want to put all their hats in one basket.’

Former Chelsea and Celtic striker Tony Cascarino on Steven Gerrard …

‘Steven’s been a quiet footballer. He’s never demanded to leave Liverpool. He’s never rattled feathers …’

Ex-Sunderland player Michael Gray on England’s Wayne Rooney …

‘We’ve got people on form. Wayne must be itching at the bit.’

Alan Brazil gets frustrated about one of his old clubs while talking to Neil Warnock …

‘Neil, with Tottenham, sometimes you hit your head against a tree. Or a wall.’

(Always good to have the tree option in the absence of a wall, Al.)

A slightly worrying one from Alvin Martin …

CALLER: ‘I think all the players should be dropped. They were a disgrace on Sunday.’

ALVIN: ‘Surely that’s throwing the baby out of the dishwater!’

Former Spurs manager David Pleat with Keys and Gray . . .

'When they did anticipate the ball and go forward, they did it quite well. They didn't just go forward hung-ho . . .'

Alan with his view on a Sunderland defender . . .

'I wouldn't touch Chimbonda with a barn door.'

Ray Houghton talking Chelsea . . .

'They just need someone to unopen the door.'

(Who unclosed it in the first place?)

The Moose chatting about the Gunners with Mike Graham . . .

MIKE: 'Arsenal seemed to develop a bit of a spine, a bit of steel to win that game.'

MOOSE: 'Yeah, but one summer does not make a swallow, or whatever it is.'

(Well, it isn't that . . .)

What's that old sportsman's saying – what happens on tour, stays on tour? Let's ask Goughie . . .

'I always believed being the player I am – what goes away, stays there.'

(That's close enough . . .)

A one-off original from Stan Collymore ...

'Louis Saha has been on and off the pitch more than an RAC man or AA bloke.'

(We'll all be using that now though, won't we?)

A caller comparing sports ...

'You ever seen a rugby player go up to a referee and scream and shout on the pitch? Their morals and principles are a lot different to footballers anyway, so you can't judge them by the same brush.'

Alan Brazil explains why he's having a bad morning ...

RONNIE: 'You're struggling with your words today!'
ALAN: 'I know. My mouth is dry – it's like a vulture's armpit!

The Moose, again ...

'Victor Obinna could barely hit a cow's backside with a barn door!'

(What happened to the banjo?)

A caller to Mike Graham ...

'We live in a country at the moment – to quote a very old saying – that is a big hat and no knickers.'

TOO MUCH INFORMATION

A cluster of clips guaranteed to have you saying: 'Yes, all right, we get the idea – no need to spell it out . . .'

A caller to Mike Graham . . .

MIKE: 'Hello, Ben. (*Sound of a flushing toilet.*) Ben, what are you doing man? What on earth is going on? Ben?'

CALLER: 'Hello.'

MIKE: 'Ben, what are you doing? You're not on the toilet, are you?'

CALLER: 'I was.'

It happens more often than you think. This is Drive's Adrian Durham . . .

ADRIAN: 'Let's speak to a Rangers fan now. Rav, how you doing?'

CALLER: 'Hi, this is actually Rav's wife. He's had to nip to the toilet quickly because he's been on hold for a while – but he's on his way back!'

ADRIAN: 'Sorry, Mrs Rav!'

CALLER: 'You're all right. If you just give him ten seconds, he'll be with you.'

An irate caller to* Kick Off *...

'I drive for a living and if I kept making blunder after blunder, I'd lose my licence. That ref is absolutely incontinent!!!'

Mike Graham reads an email from a listener with an interesting take on the Greek debt crisis ...

'Eric in Coventry says: "Mr Graham, let the Greeks suffer. A few years ago, I bought some expensive sunglasses from a shop in Crete that broke as soon as I left the shop. I complained, but all I got was thrown out of the shop by three assistants. However, on my last night, I superglued the locks of the shop door and had a poo in their doorway, quality." Well that's nice, Eric. I'm sure they'll be delighted to have you back.'

A caller to* Drive *...

ADRIAN DURHAM: 'Mike's a Liverpool fan, he wants to talk about Ince and Sturridge.'

CALLER: 'Hi guys, you all right? I'm going to have to be quick because I really need a wee.'

Another caller, with an unsavoury take on that famous old Sir Alex Ferguson quote ...

'If we do score, the last ten minutes is going to be itchy bum time.'

A shock admission from Alan Brazil ...

'I did that a few months ago out in the desert, the old belly dancing.'

George Galloway with FAR too much information ...

'At fifty-three, I'm still like a broom handle in the morning.'

(What a thought.)

Reporter John Temple at QPR v Norwich ...

'Radek Černý is replacing the injured Paddy Kenny. It appears that Kenny has a pain in his bottom.'

(He'll thank you for that, John.)

FROM THE MOUTH OF THE MOOSE (aka Sports Newsreader Ian Abrahams)

The final presenter in the *Clips of the Week*'s 'Holy Trinity' alongside Messrs Brazil and Parry, the Moose has made so many appearances on a Friday afternoon we've lost count. His contributions are generally a heady cocktail of slips of the tongue and mangled sentences, with the odd dumb remark thrown in for good measure. Yet despite this, the Moose remains one of the station's most intrepid reporters, regularly thrusting his microphone into the faces of sport's great and good and asking the questions that others dare not. Claims to fame include having never watched an episode of *The Simpsons* and possessing the world's most ridiculous laugh, yet despite these shortcomings his 100,000-plus twitter followers hang on his every word. He's as much a part of breakfast as eggy soldiers . . .

On the retirement of a true legend . . .

'Sir Alex Ferguson is bringing down the career on his career at Manchester United.'

Talking racing . . .

Ted Walsh's daughter Katy rides the much fancied Seabass. His son, Ruby, is onboard himself . . .'

Reporting from Amsterdam . . .

'The one thing I haven't seen is windmills. If I'd been here last weekend instead of at Wembley for the Cup final, it was National Windmill Day. I mean, what's that all about?

(Windmills?)

What's the name of that Welsh-Spanish bloke who played for Liverpool? Don't worry, the Moose will know . . .

'Two goal for the Reds from Rhodri Mackri – sorry, Maxi Rodriguez.'

Revealing that a footballer is thinking of switching to MMA . . .

'Cage fighting is a mixture of arts – like boxing, kick-boxing, bit of judo. He could be the first Premier League footballer to be in the KFC ring!'

(Bet Colonel Sanders is delighted!)

The trouble with the Moose is, he's just TOO football . . .

'Rory McIlroy admits he has something to prove at the Masters at Augusta, a year on from his Masters meltdown. The Northern Irishman threw away a four-goal lead a year ago on the final day.'

With transfer news . . .

'Somebody heading for the North-East is Loic Remy. He seems to be close to completing a meal.'

There'd been a lot of programmes about the fiftieth anniversary of Motown. This was Moose's contribution . . .

'How long ago was Martin Gaye's "I Heard It Through The Grapevine"?'

Revealing that one of the strikers at Euro 2012 had a sex change . . .

'A full-strength Spanish side were thumped four-nil. Carlos Martins, a Ramos own goal, a goal from the former man Helder Postiga . . .'

With an update from his beloved West Ham . . .

'Matt Taylor has been sent off – he ran half the length of the field, width wise.'

(Eh?)

Here's the Moose on the pitch pre-match at Wembley, with another of his in-depth interviews with the stars ...

THE MOOSE: 'The Manchester United players are just literally walking past me right now. In fact, let's see if we can grab a quick word with Carlos Tevez ... Carlos, good luck this afternoon!'

CARLOS TEVEZ: 'Thank you.'

THE MOOSE: 'Carlos Tevez there, saying thank you to me wishing him luck.'

Checking the weather in Dubai ...

'Is that sunshine, or is it, like, really hot sunshine? Like Caribbean sunshine, or like here – wintry sunshine? Because you can get two lots of sunshine. You can get hot sunshine, or not hot sunshine. So I was wondering – is the sunshine in Dubai hot, or is it not hot?'

(To be honest, we're beyond caring, Sunshine ...)

Talking boxing ...

'You'll remember the series of fights against Sugar Ray Lemon.'

During the London Olympics …

‘I’m Ian Abrahams live in Stratford City on Day Three of the 2012 Games – and let me tell you, the most amazing sunset over the stadium this morning.’

(You can’t beat a morning sunset.)

On Swansea’s pre-season tour of the USA …

‘Swansea lost to Columbus Crew and Colorado Rabbits …’

Announcing an amazing record …

‘Manchester City striker Emmanuel Adebayor, on loan last season at Spurs where he scored seventeen million goals …’

And discussing troubled golf great Tiger Woods …

‘Maybe all of his sort of trials and tribulations over the past few years have actually changed him a bit as a person. Maybe Tigers do change their spots.’

Maybe the reason Spurs didn’t get the Olympic stadium was because they were being a little too ambitious …

‘Spurs propose a sixteen million … sorry, a six hundred *thousand* seater stadium.’

The Moose with an interesting description of the then England manager's abilities ...

'Fabio Capello can't speak English. He hasn't bothered to learn how to speak English. Honestly, he couldn't coach a salmon how to get out of the water. You know, because they leap out of the water.'

(Yes, we get the idea, Moose. It isn't getting any better . . .)

Talking about West Ham manager Sam Allardyce ...

'Sam knows that this is going to be something that will be a rabbit around his neck, to coin a phrase.'

(And what phrase is that exactly?)

On the Olympic stadium legacy ...

'The running track would remain, but the thing is, it then stays a blue elephant . . .'

(Isn't that a Thai restaurant?)

I'LL NEVER FORGET WHAT'S-HIS-NAME

Those moments when you can see their face, but you just can't remember what they're called. Hang on, don't tell me, it's on the tip of my tongue . . .

Russell Hargreaves on* Extra Time*, chatting about Arsenal midfielder Santi Cazorla . . .

'Arsenal at home, with a bit of slick football, will probably get the job done, and I just think Sandy Cardoza is such a great signing.'

Mike Parry seems to have England's cricketers on the brain, even when he's talking about music . . .

'Did you hear Monty Pallow from Wet Wet Wet singing?'

Sports newsreader Mike Bovill . . .

'Jenson Mutton can win the Formula One World title . . .'

Alan Brazil introduces an overseas journalist …

‘Portugal take on Greece tonight, so let’s get a Greek point of view from the Greek daily newspaper *Elether, Eletherith Taipos* – goodness me, I hope I pronounced that right. Let’s say a very good morning to George, Geo, Georg-, Kapop – Ka- oh, hold on … George, Ge-orge Kapopoulos. George, I’m sorry. I’m struggling – I always have struggled with Greek names, George. Good morning.’

GEORGE: ‘Good morning. You didn’t do too bad, actually.’

(Didn’t do too bad???)

Alan Brazil takes us back to his youth …

ALAN: ‘Once a scout, always a scout. Do you know who the Head of the Scouts is at the moment?

RONNIE IRANI: ‘Go on …’

ALAN: ‘Err, what’s-his-name? Bear Grease.’

A Chelsea fan nominates his next choice of manager …

‘Personally, it’s Guus Higgin all day for me …’

And an Arsenal fan on Drive discussing their boss …

‘Arsene Vagner’s done a good job.’

Newsreader Lisa O'Sullivan . . .

'It was a final home game for David Scholes who announced his retirement for a second time yesterday.'

Mike Parry chatting about actress Zoe Lucker and her dance partner . . .

'She was on *Footballers' Wives*, so you can imagine how glamorous she would be, to be in that show. And as you rightly say, Anton Dec is one of the best-known figures on *Strictly Come Dancing*.'

(Think he meant Anton Du Beke – although if you were looking for a quicker way to say Ant & Dec . . .)

Mark Saggers struggling with a manager's name . . .

'Spurs, just three points behind Manchester City at the top of the Premier League – Harry Redknopp's not getting carried away.'

This is Chelsea great Ron Harris talking about his former club . . .

'Whether it's the FA Cup or League Cup or whatever, I think the Chelsea players will be up for it anyway. I'm sure Raffle Benitez will.'

(I don't think the club sold a lot of tickets.)

A caller to Breakfast on Theo Walcott ... that's WalcoTT

'Good morning, I want to talk about Theo Wallcock. I think Theo Willcock should stay ...'

Lisa O'Sullivan again, this time looking ahead to the PFA Awards ...

'Bale and Hazard are also in the running for Young Player of the Year, alongside Christian Ben-tekker and Romelu Lugluku ...'

This caller's clearly a big England fan ...

'If you look at the England team, Glen Johnson, Wade Rooney, Gary Barry ...'

Richard Keys drops a 'Bullock' while introducing a Scottish rugby legend ...

'Seventeen days now until the Rugby World Cup finals and this morning we're talking Scotland with Gordon Bollock. Morning, Gordon.'

Alan trying to recall the name of a famous French rugby player ...

'He was on the telly – the French game. Serge, Serge Beh-Beh-Beh-Ben-Be-Be Benoit, BESSON! Nice guy.'

(Yes, and so is Serge Betsen.)

We all remember Brian Clough's nickname 'Old Big 'Ed', don't we? Not Alan . . .

'"Psycho" Stuart Pearce spent eight years under Cloughie at Nottingham Forest, and was there when he left football for good following relegation. Pearce said "Old Big Ears's" magic rubbed off on him . . .'

Lisa O'Sullivan on F1 . . .

'Formula One boss Bertie . . . Bert . . . Bernie Ecclestone . . .'

(You can see why he shortened it to just Bernie . . .)

We've often wondered who Goughie's favourite umpire was . . .

'Charlie Adam, to be fair to him, hasn't said a dickie bow.'

(Dickie Bow, of course . . .)

Ronnie Irani reads an email . . .

'Morning chaps. My daughter's called Hale – after Hale Berry.'

(. . . And, no doubt, Hale's Comet, Bill Hale and Hale Mills.)

Here's Alan Brazil and Ronnie Irani – and if you can't pronounce someone's name, just keep having a punt until you get roughly in the vicinity ...

ALAN: Ex-Schalke, Fulham and Germany Under-21, back now at St Pauli in the Bundesliga, delighted to welcome to the morning show, Maurice Voltz. Moreetz, how are you, Moritz?
RONNIE: 'Morning, Smoritz!'

Alan Brazil going through the newspapers with Ronnie and newsreader Faye Carruthers – and you wonder why Al never became a showbiz correspondent ...

ALAN: 'In the *Mirror* this morning – it's Jennifer Lopez and . . .'
FAYE: 'No, that's not Jennifer Lopez!'
ALAN: 'Who is it?'
FAYE: 'Paula Abdul!'
ALAN: 'Paula Abdul – the dancer, right?'
RONNIE: 'She's a singer!'
ALAN: 'Dancer as well, she used to dance.'
FAYE: 'And now a judge on the *X Factor*.'
ALAN: 'And who's Lewis's bird? What's her name?
FAYE: 'Nicole Scherzinger.'
ALAN: 'Scherzinger, that's right.'

Here's journalist Steve Curry, who is clearly down with the kids . . .

'The venue boasts the likes of Prince Harry, Robert De Niro, Jay-Zed . . .'

(Steve's got 99 problems and one of them is pronouncing Jay-Z.)

Big Alan watching Stoke v Chelsea . . .

'Pennant and Etherington are working hard and so is Kenrin, Kenwhite Road, er, Kenwright Jones.'

(Or even his brother Kenwyne.)

Journalist Steve Curry listing Newcastle's options at centre-forward . . .

'Albert Luque, Michael Owen, Oberfemur Martins . . .'

(Think Oberfemur has a thigh injury.)

WHEN 2 + 2 = 5

Statistics play a major part in sport, but the combination of live radio and mental arithmetic sometimes challenges the best of us. These are the moments when the numbers just didn't stack up . . .

Transfer Tavern *host Neil Ashton . . .*

'Our poll on the website is, should Wayne Rooney stay or go? Fifty-two per cent at the moment are saying that Rooney should stay – and the other forty-eight per cent say that Wayne Rooney should remain at Manchester United.'

(Pretty unanimous, then.)

Stan Collymore . . .

'Let's not forget, this isn't a lad that's gone off the rails. This is a lad that's scored ninety goals in his last three games.'

(You have to admit, that's prolific.)

Alan Brazil on Arsenal's record-breaking striker . . .

'Thierry Henry scored his one hundred and fifty-oneth league goal . . .'

Maths isn't the Moose's strong point either ...

'Two down, three to go, as Manchester United chase the Quadruple.'

Ronnie Irani ...

'The Cardiff owner Vincent Tan is a billionaire. He's worth, like, eight hundred and fifty million pounds!'

Mike Parry with an interesting fact on the stadium in Almaty, where England played Kazakhstan ...

'The stadium is fifty years old and the pitch has never been replaced in fifty-nine years.'

And Mike's legendary maths skills have not improved sadly ...

'Andy, you can do that easy in your head. Two multiplied by 6, the first two numbers, 25 right, 3s into 25 is 8 – that leaves 2 over, 25 again, so that must be an 8. No wait, sorry, sorry, sorry I can do it in my head. Three into 25 is 8, 2 over, 3 and 2, no hang on.'

(We'll get back to you, Mike.)

Micky Quinn ...

'Liverpool got at Man United in the second half when Sturridge came on. It changed the possession stats at one point to seventy-seven per cent, thirty-three per cent.'

Presenter Ian Collins taking us back to school times tables ...

'I've never forgotten them ... part of it is poetic, remembering them – "four fours are four", "five fives are five ... "'

The Moose again ...

'Arsenal have made a forty million and one pound bid for Luis Suarez – so a forty-one million pound bid, basically ...'

January always seems like a long month. Mike explains why ...

'Schools have until the thirty-third of January ...'

Darren Gough ...

'Lampard had a brilliant season once again – two hundred and three goals.'

(And Chelsea wanted to sell him?!)

Alan Brazil looking to get a job with Opta . . .

'Paul Scholes made seventy-five passes in the first half against Liverpool, completing ninety-three of them – which is ninety-seven per cent.'

The Moose on the world's fastest man . . .

'Usain Bolt has issued himself a challenge – he wants to run nine point four seconds for the hundred metres, and nine seconds dead for the two hundred metres. He might be able to do that as well.'

(He's quick, but not that quick.)

Alan on Blackburn shipping goals . . .

'Last four games, they lost three-nil to Wigan, lost three-one to Liverpool, lost five-three to United and they lost three-two to Portsmouth. Now it doesn't take a rocket scientist to add them up. That's twelve, isn't it – twelve goals in four games?'

(We reckon a rocket scientist might have come up with the correct answer of fourteen.)

Andy Gray at Euro 2012 . . .

'I'm looking out the window and there's about twelve Russian supporters with a ball, having a five-a-side . . .'

We're guessing maths wasn't Ray Parlour's strong point at school ...

'Moose, you speak to a lot of the fans – is it split? You know, fifty per cent want him to leave and fifty want to keep him? Or is it the other way round?'

The Moose with Champions League news ...

'Elsewhere last night, Raul scored a record breaking goal as Schalke beat Valencia one-one.'

If our cricket commentator Jack Bannister ever needs a stats man to work alongside him, then Quinny is his man ...

'They are a fantastic team, in their last eleven Tests they've won eleven and drawn three.'

Alan Brazil has goal news ...

'Stevenage three, Pompey, sorry, Peterborough four – excuse me, Posh. Stevenage three, Peterborough one after extra-time.'

(That's cleared that up.)

Amazing news from Stan Collymore at the Etihad ...

'Manchester City destroyed Norwich – thirty-five second-half goals for City!'

(We'll definitely watch that on Match of the Day.)

OBVIOUS (as in Stating the Bleedin' . . .)

A cornerstone of sports broadcasting throughout the years, here's a collection of statements that didn't need making and for which answers were not required . . .

The Moose with the lowdown on Andy Murray's upcoming Wimbledon opponent . . .

'His full name is Robert Bradley Kendrick, he's twenty-nine and was born in Fresno, California. He's the youngest of four kids – all the other three are older . . .'

Match reporter Simon Humphries with some pre-match injury news . . .

'DJ Campbell has been sent home ill – with illness.'

Presenter Alvin Martin reads an email . . .

'"Hi, Alvin. The unique thing about me is my Christian name – Vale. As far as I know, there are only two other people in the UK with the same name." Who's that from? Oh, it's from Vale.'

The Moose again …

'Obviously, the new Wembley – it's not the old Wembley.'

England Under-20s coach, Peter Taylor …

'What I saw in Holland and what I know in Germany is that the majority of people there are Dutch in Holland – and German in Germany.'

Ray Parlour recalling Arsenal's 'Invincibles' on* Breakfast *…

'I remember in the unbeaten season, the last six games were the most pressurised games you'll ever be involved in because … we were under pressure!'

This is the Moose, midway through the rugby …

'Jonathan Sexton, Brian O'Driscoll and Tom Croft with the three first-half unanswered tries. Second-half commentary to come – after half-time.'

Jason Cundy on winter breaks …

'I don't think a winter break would work for the reasons I'm about to give. One: When would you have a winter break?'

(Autumn?)

Andy Townsend's got a question for our film reviewer . . .

'Now let's move on to *Snakes on a Plane*. What's that about?

(Goats on a Boat?)

Fisherman's Blues' *Nigel Botherway chats to a caller . . .*

NIGEL: 'Usually I find with the roach-bream hybrids, the anal fin is often the giveaway.'
CALLER: 'The anal fin? Is that under the belly at the back?'

(No, it's on its forehead! Where do you think it is?)

It's tough to argue with this caller . . .

'There's no point flogging a dead horse for fifty years. If you flog a dead horse for fifty years, it will end up dead!'

Alan Brazil talks golf . . .

'Fredrik Jacobson – one over, great putt there. Swedes again! Where do they get them from, the Swedes?'

(Sweden?)

Stan Collymore ...

'Welcome back to Ewood Park – it's ten to six. You're well ensconced in your vehicular ... er ... vehicles.'

(What other type is there?)

Mike Parry chatting to a caller about his migraine headaches ...

MIKE: 'So physically, it's as though somebody's trying to push your eye out of its socket?'
CALLER: 'That's right.'
MIKE: 'Is it painful?'

The Moose talking cricket ...

'When I was a kid, I used to go down to Lord's for the old Sunday League, you remember that? Basically the Sunday League used to be on a Sunday.'

Stan Collymore with his match report ...

'Darren Bent could have doubled the lead – which I'm sure would have made a difference to the scoreline.'

The Moose recalling a meeting with football's most powerful man ...

'I spoke to Sepp Blatter on the day we won the bid in Singapore. I cornered him – in a corner.'

OO-ER MISSUS!

Innuendo. Not the Brazilian striker Harry's been trying to sign for QPR, just a bit of old-school smut. Enjoy . . .

Alan Brazil chatting to former England rugby coach, Dick Best . . .

'Dick, when I see Jonny Wilkinson being carried off the field and people immediately writing him off, that hurts me. That really hurts me, Dick.'

Andy Townsend with a shock admission . . .

'I didn't say it was going to happen, because I haven't got crystal balls.'

Mike Parry with a competition . . .

'We test how much of a man you really are. Wow – fancy having your manhood put to the test like this.'

Ray Stubbs and Alvin Martin discussing Jose Mourinho . . .

RAY: 'When he walks into the room, he commands respect. The man has charisma.'

ALVIN: 'So do you, Ray. As soon as you walk into a room, I stand to attention.'

Cricket correspondent Jack Bannister giving details of West Indies' Ramnaresh Sarwan being struck by the ball during the second Test . . .

'He's just been pole-axed – and when people gather round someone who's been hit at ninety miles an hour, they either look very concerned or start laughing. And they're laughing, so you can guess where he got hit – the proverbials. But it's always a source of mystery to me as to why, because that can actually cause longer term damage than if you get one on the helmet.'

Alan Brazil and Ronnie Irani talk cycling . . .

ALAN: 'Money will be no problem, but have they got the expertise to encourage more and more kids to be stars in four years' time?'

RONNIE: 'Yeah, you'll just have to get your Chopper out, Al.'

Alan probably needed to come up with a better way to describe Tranmere Rovers fans to our Merseyside correspondent, Graham Beecroft . . .

BEEKY: 'You try and name any Tranmere Rovers players. They haven't got any ex-top pros or anything like that in their side.'

ALAN: 'Beeky, you are a Tranny . . .'

Mike Parry on a well-known manager …

'Harry Redknobb will eventually get his man, he always does.'

Racing expert Derek 'Tommo' Thompson and Alan talking racing …

ALAN: 'Hell of a jockey, Richard Johnson.'
TOMMO: 'Hell of a Johnson!'

(Who knew?)

A caller to Stan Collymore …

'I remember in the old days, Clive Thomas used to blow the referee – sorry, his whistle!'

Mike Parry with shock political news …

'The big story today, away from football, is the unveiling of Chancellor Osborne's package.'

Jason Cundy on footballers' flashy cars …

'You can't criticise someone for spending their own money. They've earned it. It wouldn't be my taste. I wouldn't want a diamond encrusted knob …'

Mike Parry chatting to* Fisherman's Blues' *Nigel Botherway . . .

NIGEL: 'I've got an email from Jean. "I want to marry a fisherman," she says. Great shout. What do you reckon, Mike?'

MIKE: 'Well, there's still a vacancy for the first Mrs Parry – so I'd better get me rod out!'

A corker from Alan . . .

'Good morning and welcome to the Alan Brazil *Sports Breakfast* with guest co-host, former England all-rounder, Dominic Cock.'

And once Alan had got his name right and they got chatting, things got even more interesting . . .

DOMINIC: 'I'm on a bit of a detox at the moment . . .'

ALAN: 'Oh, really?'

DOMINIC: 'It's a nine-day detox which includes protein milkshakes.'

ALAN: 'Earlier on, you were drooling over my ginger nuts!'

Keith Arthur, at it again on* Fisherman's Blues *. . .

'I bet you enjoy watching that last six inches of your rod wang round.'

An image you'd rather not dwell on ...

'I'm Russell Hargreaves here on *Extra Time* with Lynsey Hooper and Toby Gilles back inside me in the studio ...'

(What a thought.)

Mike Parry with a shock confession ...

'I'm getting mangled here, because my equipment's a bit dodgy.'

Alan Brazil on his favourite film ...

ALAN: 'For me, *The Penis* was one of the best films. If you've not seen that, watch *The Penis*. Magnificent.'

RONNIE: 'The what, Al? Oh, *The Pianist*.'

Golf correspondent Rupert Bell reveals just how close he gets to the top players on the tour ...

'Rory McIlroy is on the eighteenth with his prodigious length ...'

Mark Saggers was no fan of the then Liverpool boss ...

'I don't like Rafa Benitez as a manager, but his package is a little bit different to Carlos Tevez's.'

And if you've ever wondered what Mike Parry gets up to after a show . . .

'I flashed quite a lot of drivers on the motorway yesterday as you know . . .'

Let's go route one with Welsh rugby legend Gareth Edwards on Breakfast . . .

ALAN BRAZIL: 'Of course, we are building up to the Rugby World Cup in New Zealand. I don't know if our next guest is going down – I hope so. Wales's legendary scrum-half Gareth Edwards joins us now. Gareth, good morning!'

GARETH: 'Good morning, Alan. Crikey, you've got me standing up already first thing in the morning!'

Journalist Steve Curry remembers just how close the relationship was between players and journalists in the old days . . .

'When I was in my twenties and the players were contemporaries, we used to mate together.'

(You'd struggle to keep that out of the papers nowadays.)

This is Stan Collymore . . .

'You don't have to go out and give Arsene Wenger a woody!'

(We wouldn't dream of it.)

The Moose looking ahead to the big fight . . .

'The politics of boxing means it doesn't always happen. But I suppose by calling him a chicken, you're trying to get under his manhood.'

Alan Brazil on a big day at Twickenham . . .

'In the rugby, we've got two massive semis coming up.'

This is Tony Incenzo reporting from Brighton v Liverpool . . .

'Brighton nil, Liverpool one, but Brighton starting the second half with real dynamite in their shorts.'

(Must be the little blue – and white striped – pills.)

THE MIGHTY QUINN

Much loved, well-travelled striker for the likes of Newcastle, Coventry, Portsmouth and PAOK Thessaloniki, 'Quinny' combines a natural Scouse wit with undoubted football knowledge – but is prone to the odd *faux pas*. Although, as you'll discover, that's not what he'd call it himself . . .

Former Newcastle and Coventry striker turned talkSPORT presenter Micky Quinn discusses the first man on the moon, Neil Armstrong . . .

'I remember his quote: "One small step for mankind."'

(Clearly you don't, Mick . . .)

This is probably not the best turn of phrase to use to boxer James DeGale . . .

'You're exciting to watch, James – when can the public next see you back on the canvas?'

(As opposed to 'on your back on the canvas'.)

Turning into Mystic Mick when talking about Norwich . . .

'They're unbeaten in their next three games.'

Recalling his playing career . . .

'After the first game of the season, I tell you, I was breathing through my backside – sweating profoundly.'

With co-host Mark Saggers, watching Usain Bolt on TV while they are on air . . .

QUINNY: 'I just clocked Usain Bolt's race there, Mark.'
SAGGERS: 'How far behind was he?'
QUINNY: 'Well for him, about a mile.'

(That's some feat in a 100 metre race, Mick!)

Looking ahead to the big game . . .

'Both sides are looking to avenge five-nil defeats in their opening fistures.'

(Sounds painful.)

On Liverpool's new signing . . .

'It's Nuri Sahin on a season-long loan deal – subject to the player passing a medal.'

(That's worse than a kidney stone.)

Chatting to Crawley manager Steve Evans about new loan signing Sanchez Watt ...

QUINNY: 'Will he be able to understand your Scottish accent, Steve? Ha ha!'

STEVE: 'Ha!'

QUINNY: 'What nationality is the kid?'

STEVE: 'He's from Hackney.

THAT'S EASY FOR YOU TO SAY

To quote the late great Ronnie Barker, here's a hodge-podge of presenters and listeners 'pisspronouncing their worms' . . .

Jason Cundy alerted us to an event for private detectives we didn't even know existed . . .

'Let's get an update from Richard Fleming at the World Snooper Championships in York.'

Jason again, looking ahead to a special Wimbledon edition of* My Sporting Life *. . .

'The show includes the story of the Crazy Gang's route to the FA Cup final, when Liverpool got caught out, and some never-heard-before antidotes.'

The Times's *football editor, Tony Evans . . .*

'When talking to the people at the highest level at Liverpool a couple of months ago, they were saying they wanted big money for Suarez. They saw him as being more than just a player – as more symbollock.'

Russell Hargreaves reads an email ...

'Rob Effort says, "What about Kyle Walker? Surprised he wasn't nominated for Young Player of the Year. Hashslag, er, HashTAG Unsung Hero."'

This is Ray Parlour on the Potters ...

'I think Stoke are in that situation where they're playing for nothing – and players do get lacksadaisy.'

World football expert Gabriele Marcotti ...

'Do you really think that that plays such a big fart? Sorry, *part* ...'

Mike Parry, having just played a festive classic ...

'... and that is Paul McCartney and 'Simply Having a Lovely Christmas Time'. Paul McCartney is one of my favourite arses of all time!'

If you've been to an Aldershot game, how do you describe it in the past tense? Here's UFO expert Nick Pope nailing it ...

'The first football match I ever went to was at Aldershat ...'

Some lists of names don't suit the 'your' treatment, as former Chelsea and Manchester United midfielder Ray Wilkins proves here . . .

'It was a little bit difficult at the start of the season when you're losing players like your Decos, your Joe Coles – your Ballacks.'

Rick Kelsey with the sports news . . .

'Football's governing body FIFA has confirmed a game between Argentina and Nigeria played earlier this month is being investigated for possible Max Fitching . . .'

Jason Cundy, who finds it hard to hide just what a big* Star Trek *fan he is . . .

'Pakistani cricketers Salman Butt and Mohammad Asif have been found guilty of spock-fixing.'

(Beamer me up, Scotty.)

NEW BALLS, PLEASE . . .

For some reason, tennis is second only to football in generating clips. Probably a combination of tricky-to-pronounce names and technical jargon. Alan Brazil serves first, after a session on the barley water, by the look of things . . .

Alan Brazil introducing one of Britain's top tennis players . . .

'We're gonna hear from Alex Bug-Bog-Bogdanovic in a moment. In fact, can we hear from Alex Bug-Bugda-Bogdanovic now.'

(We think he may have Bug-Bugda-Bogged off, Al.)

And Alan wasn't the only one struggling with his name. Here's the Moose . . .

'Andy Murray has passed Alex Bogalogalof in the second round of the Japan Open.'

Alan again, on women's tennis . . .

'Veteran Lindsay Davenport – I think she's a mum now as well. Or she's had her knees done.'

(It's one of the two, we're sure.)

Tennis correspondent Dave Luddy . . .

'Federer's going to play an opponent who's world ranked at 152 and he may be perplexed at the start because his opponent has two hands on both sides . . .'

(Great for the quadruple-handed backhand.)

Alan talking tennis with former Davis Cup player Barry Cowan . . .

'What about Andy Murray, then? His next opponent should be fairly straightforward now Ivan Lendly is looking after him.'

(Ivan Lendly?)

The Moose has some tennis news . . .

'Andy Murray will play in the last sixteen of the Miami Masters in Miami today.'

(Really? We thought it was in Chelmsford.)

Ian Danter struggling with the name of 2013 Wimbledon giantkiller Sergiy Stakhovsky . . .

'Let's reflect on Federer's departure to the qualifier Sergiy Shit-off-ski . . .'

Lisa O'Sullivan reporting from Wimbledon . . .

'It's about to get underway on court number one. The girls are knocking up Laura Robson.'

Former tennis star Barry Cowan on Breakfast . . .

RONNIE IRANI: 'It says here £22 million has been spent by the LTA on elite player development.'

BARRY: 'It's not that much a year.'

RONNIE: 'How does it compare to other nations – is that a lot of money or not?'

BARRY: 'Well, certainly if we compare Britain to France – now that's the model we should be copying.'

RONNIE: 'How much do they spend?'

BARRY: 'I don't know.'

Mike Parry struggling with a top tennis player's name . . .

MIKE: 'The tennis writers are saying that maybe the big four's gone now – maybe it's now time for people like, what's-his-name? Del Tosso?

ALAN: 'Del Potro!'

MIKE: 'Del Potro, thank you.'

Keys and Gray, chatting to former British number one Andrew Castle . . .

RICHARD: 'If you hadn't beaten Mats Wilander, how different do you think your life would have been?'

ANDREW: 'I lost to him.'

LET'S HEAR FROM THE EXPERTS

talkSPORT is fortunate to be able to call on a glittering array of sporting talent past and present – as well as a coterie of celebrated journalists and authors – to add credibility and insight to any debate. But thankfully, even the gurus get it wrong now and again. Hence this section . . .

The Mirror's John Cross on* Breakfast*, getting down with the kids . . .

'It's been a funny season for Crewe. They've been so consistent, so solid Crewe.'

Former Southampton defender Mark Dennis . . .

'That's all it's about, one word: Man management.'

Journalist Sophie Nicolau on* Extra Time*, talking Becks . . .

'Regardless of what people think about David Beckham, he's had a huge impact on the game here and it's going to take a very special player to come in and be able to carry the mantelpiece.'

Ray Houghton's a lot older than he looks ...

'I watched a game I was involved in the other night – it was the title decider between Liverpool and Arsenal in 1889.'

Andy Gray, with a question for former Wolves and City midfielder Steve Daley ...

ANDY: 'How did you play in the Cup final in '74?'
STEVE: 'How did I play?'
ANDY: 'Yeah, come on?'
STEVE: 'In the '74 Cup final?'
ANDY: 'Yeah ...'
STEVE: 'I didn't!'

Some shock news from our South American correspondent Tim Vickery ...

'There is a kind of industry here in Brazil of girls who are trying to get footballers pregnant.'

Cricket correspondent Jack Bannister with news that suggests Trent Bridge needs to take a close look at its medical procedures ...

'Rahim took a very nasty blow to his left eye through his helmet. He's been taken to hospital strapped to an ambulance.'

Legendary racing tipster Derek Thompson on* Breakfast *. . .

ALAN: 'Tommo. The tennis at Wimbledon. Are you there? Have you been yet?'

TOMMO: 'I'd love to, Al, but I'm going to Sheffield Greyhound Stadium tonight.'

(The next best thing. Try gravy on your strawberries and cream.)

Then Cardiff youth coach Neil Ardley tells us something we didn't know about Arsenal new boy, Aaron Ramsey . . .

'In certain games when the chips are down he's the one player that can pick up the mantelpiece and drive everyone else around him on.'

(Is that the same mantelpiece David Beckham was carrying in Los Angeles?)

The prize for most repetitions of the phrase 'open side flanker' goes to former England prop, Jeff Probyn . . .

'England desperately need an open side flanker. They haven't got an open side flanker. They are making do with Chris Robshaw – but he's not an open side. England need a true open side flanker. We need to see an open side flanker in the England squad playing proper rugby.'

(Hope that's not rhyming slang?)

Ray Parlour ...

'West Ham have had a very good season under Sam Ambulance.'

Sam Matterface getting a touch confused over the Open's legendary Claret Jug ...

'Bobby Locke, Gary Player and Louis Oosthuizen – the three South Africans, apart from Gary Player, to have lifted the Carrot.'

Former Norwich manager John Deehan, talking Wigan ...

'I'm not so sure if they'll have their strongest team out. I think the boy Alcatraz has been struggling.'

Jason Cundy on Chelsea's problems behind the scenes ...

'As a football club you have to stick together and hopefully everyone pulls together and results go your way. Don't start picking battles and trying to dismember the squad.'

Ronnie Irani talking up Breakfast guest Dave 'Harry' Bassett ...

'We're going to have relegation specialist Dave Bassett joining us in the studio.'

(I'm sure he was delighted with that description, Ronnie.)

When Dave Bassett did come on, he had an interesting question for Gillingham Chairman Paul Scally . . .

'Hello Paul, Aitch here. When I spoke to you after you came out the Championship, the club was on a rockety situation. I know you had a lot of thoughts – now you seem to have it back on the basis.'

(No, we've no idea either.)

Extra Time's *Russell Hargreaves . . .*

RUSSELL: 'Time to take a look at continental football from across the weekend with one of our resident experts, Kevin Hatchard. Kev, good morning mate – how's your weekend been?'

KEVIN: 'Very good thank you, very enjoyable. Plenty of football as always.'

RUSSELL: 'Absolutely, we know you like to feast on the round balls.'

Australia rugby legend Michael Lynagh, going a bit 'Star Wars' on Breakfast . . .

ALAN BRAZIL: 'Michael, what sort of game will the Lions get from Western Force?'

MICHAEL: 'The Force will be strong.'

Ex-Northern Ireland manager Nigel Worthington suggesting how England should approach their game against Italy . . .

'I think they've got to go at it a little bit more and throw caution to the wind – in a cautious way.'

(Thanks for that, Nige.)

Former Wimbledon striker John Fashanu on* Breakfast *. . .

ALAN: 'John, were you surprised when Mark McGhee was sacked?'

JOHN: 'I was very surprised, *very* surprised. But in football nothing surprises us anymore . . .'

Here's betting guru Mark Pearson on* Breakfast *. . .

'Hairy Redknapp is the 5/4 favourite to be the next England manager.'

(Perhaps Sky's Gary Cotterill could give him a trim through his car window on deadline day.)

Journalist Steve Curry on* Breakfast *– and if you're going to mispronounce this player's name, this probably isn't the best way to do it . . .

CURRY: 'Villa weren't a team filled with foreigners, they had good English players. Ashley Young, Milner, Ag-Ag . . .'

RONNIE IRANI: 'Agbonlahor?'

CURRY: 'Agbanglahor.'

Former West Ham and Celtic striker John Hartson, on Rangers' David Weir . . .

'He was way off Gary Hooper. He [Weir] showed really yesterday that his legs have gone – and it's time to hang them up.'

Not a lot of people realise that QPR coach and talkSPORT pundit, Marc Bircham is a top magician . . .

'It's different in the Premier League now because of the foreign influence. You just levitate to people who speak your own language or who are from the same country.'

This was Spurs' assistant manager Kevin Bond on Breakfast – and we're all for a team being ambitious but we think this might be pushing it a bit . . .

'Our aim at the start of the season is to finish as high as possible – higher than the top four if we can.'

Former Everton keeper Neville Southall on his beloved Blues . . .

'We just keep spending. He's made the decision to go "actually, we can't do it anymore". Now is that a sensible solution, really? Or should he just go and buy ten or fifteen million people?'

(Might be difficult to keep them all happy in a 25-man squad.)

Sam Fleet at Cardiff v Leicester for talkSPORT ...

'Interesting symmetry in the kit tonight, if you're interested. Cardiff, blue shirts, white shorts, er, shirts, er, blue shirts, white shorts and blue socks. Leicester – white shirts, blue ... shorts and white socks, if you follow me.'

(Not really.)

Shocking news from the Hawthorns from Graham Beecroft ...

'West Brom took the lead, Peter Odemwingie going through – he was brought down by referee Jan Mucha.'

(Hope he gave himself a red card.)

Ex-Ireland midfielder and talkSPORT presenter Matt Holland on the World Cup play-offs ...

'We haven't got a great play-off record, so when the draw was made it was the best we could hope for. To have the second leg second is great.'

(True, would have been much harder to play the second leg first.)

WHAT I MEANT TO SAY WAS . . .

Every talkSPORT presenter, travel reporter and overwrought caller has, at one time, said something that just didn't come out as planned. These are a few memorable examples . . .

Mike Parry turns his attention to a versatile household staple . . .

'Look at Bicarbonate of Sober, there are books about its many uses.'

Georgie Bingham seems to have a low opinion of the natives of Swansea and Bradford . . .

'All eyes turn to Wembley for the League Cup final this afternoon. Ninety thousand odd people expected here.'

Jason Cundy with news of a surprise at Wimbledon . . .

'This is one of the biggest shocks I can remember. Darcis the Belgium has knocked out Rafa Nadal – and is punching the crowd in celebration!'

Darren Gough makes an interesting point ...

'There are people who'd give their right leg to be a professional footballer.'

Beaky on the England manager–captain relationship ...

'We now know that the Sven–David Beckham thing is "you scratch your back, I'll scratch my back".'

(So they're both just scratching their own backs, basically.)

Fisherman's Blues' *Nigel Botherway* ...

'They want to learn how to be better at fishing. You know what kids are like, you can't take away that competitive elephant.'

Georgie Bingham again ...

'Gareth Bale strikes me as a man who likes to go home to Wales to his mum, who likes to play in the Premier League.'

(Who knew? Wonder if old Ma Bale is as good as her boy?)

Ronnie Irani goes through the papers with Alan Brazil ...

RONNIE: 'This is one of the headlines in the *Daily Express* this morning: "WHY PEOPLE THINK A HOTEL BREAK IS A STEAL". Apparently, Britain is becoming a nation of pretty thieves ...'
ALAN: 'Petty thieves!!!!'

An annoyed caller . . .

'I've tried to find work – but at the minute this country is going to hell in a hanging basket.'

Mark Saggers tells us about the Women's Olympic football . . .

'The football starts here today at the Olympics. The squad's made up of sixteen women and two Scots.'

(Were they wearing kilts?)

Here's our Adam with some surprising travel news . . .

'Disruption continues between Birmingham New Street and Sheffield due to a deranged train.'

Mike Parry on Manchester City . . .

'The City fans have been promised that the team will change from a sow's purse into a pig's ear.'

A caller to Drive . . .

'Afternoon guys. I'm somewhat caught between a devil and a hard rock . . .'

Alan Brazil previewing an upcoming guest, author Gershon Portnoi and his excellent talkSPORT book* Ashes, Clashes and Bushy Taches *– although it doesn't quite come out that way …

'Plenty still to come on the Alan Brazil *Sports Breakfast* this morning, including Gershwyn Port-noir, author of *Ashes, Clashes and Bushy Tails* …'

Mike Parry with a question …

'Has Robbie Keane ever set on fire any team that he's played for?'

(Imagine that would be at least a three-game ban, Mike.)

Here's a caller to Keys and Gray …

'If they set a precedent by starting to overturn these decisions, they're opening a huge can of wormholes …'

Alan Brazil invented a new word to describe going to Wembley …

'Let's hear from *Daily Mail* football writer Steve Curry with his favourite Wembling moment.'

Micky Quinn on clubs new to the top division . . .

'Are fans of promoted clubs feeling good ahead of the new season in the Premier League? Or, judging by these callers – is there a little pre-Susan gloom?'

(Didn't Dr Karl Kennedy from Neighbours suffer from pre-Susan gloom?)

Adrian Durham with an email . . .

'Dom in Manchester says it doesn't take a rocket surgeon to see that the climate and seasons are changing.'

(And it doesn't take a rocket scientist to realise that he meant 'rocket scientist'.)

Alan Brazil on England v Spain . . .

'Is Cesc right? Has England's win pampered over the cracks?'

COMPETITION TIME

Take the high-pressure elements of live radio, tricky questions and the lure of a fantastic prize, and it's no wonder that sometimes things go horribly wrong. Making a cameo appearance in this collection of quiz nightmares is *Drive* co-host Darren Gough. An England fast bowling legend, 'Goughie' has made the transition from cricket star to showbiz icon fairly effortlessly. Skittling Aussies and gliding across the dancefloor may have come easily to him, but reading out loud has been known to stump him on the odd occasion ...

Mike Parry setting up a competition ...

'You've got thirty seconds – and remember, every question is an answer. Let's go!'

(How does that work?)

Ray Houghton with a cricket competition ...

'You'll need to hit your opponent out of the ground for your chance to pee pitchside.'

(One for the Ashes-winning England boys at The Oval.)

Jason Cundy reflecting on a career highlight . . .

'You asked if I'd ever won a talent competition. Well, when I was eighteen, in a local nightclub in Streatham called Studios, I won Mr Wet Boxer Shorts.'

(You can smell the ammonia from here.)

Alan Brazil asking the quiz questions on* Breakfast *. . .

ALAN: 'Who was Superman's alter ego?'
CALLER: 'Doctor No?'

Mike with a question about Prince Harry's ex-girlfriend . . .

MIKE: 'Chelsea Davey goes out with one of England's most eligible bachelors – who is it?'
CALLER: 'Oh . . . I'll say . . . um . . . er.'
MIKE: 'Come on, apart from me, who is one of Britain's most eligible bachelors?'
CALLER: 'I don't know! Darren Bent?'

Presenter Ian Wright on the United–Liverpool game with one of our easier competition questions . . .

'What was the score when it was three-one?'

X Factor ***singer*** **Olly Murs,** ***co-presenting*** **Breakfast** ***with*** **Alan** ***Brazil, setting the questions in a competition for an 'expert' on the*** **Who** ***...***

OLLY: 'Who was the band's original bass player?

CALLER: 'Erm ... ohhh ... pfff ... Keith Moon?'

OLLY: 'No, that was John Entwistle. Who worked in a sheet metal factory and made the band's guitars?'

CALLER: 'Pete Townshend.'

OLLY: 'No, Roger Daltrey. Who wrote the band's first hit "I Can't Explain"?'

CALLER: 'Ermmmm ... Keith Moon.'

OLLY: 'No. That was Pete Townshend. Who directed the movie version of *Tommy*?

CALLER: 'Roger Daltrey.'

OLLY: 'No. Ken Russell. Who did the band support in their first US tour in 1967?'

CALLER: 'Ooffff ... The Stones?'

OLLY: 'No, Herman's Hermits. Who was born in Wembley on 23 August 1946?'

CALLER: 'Roger Daltrey.'

OLLY: 'No, it was Keith Moon. Who wrote the song "Highbury Highs" for the ground's farewell ceremony?

CALLER: 'Roger Daltrey.'

OLLY: 'Wahayyyyyyyy!! You got one right!!!'

Mike Parry with a nice simple clue to a question in a music competition . . .

'Her debut album title shares part of its name with a transparent liquid which is a common organic solvent used in painting and decorating – what is it?'

(Aw, you've given it away now, Mike!)

Mike Parry with a tough one . . .

'Who was the lead singer of the very, very successful Seventies-slash-Eighties group, The Pretenders' Chrissy Hynde?'

(Ooh, don't tell us . . .)

Ronnie Irani with another brainteaser . . .

'How many daughters does Alan have? I must admit – all three of them are beautiful.'

Alan Brazil goes sci-fi . . .

'Which comedy double act were *Star Wars* robots C-3PO and Ar-tee-Do-too . . ?'

***Adrian Durham and Darren Gough with a competition about action movie* The Expendables 2. *That's* The Expendables . . .**

ADRIAN: 'On 16 August, *The Expendables Two* is exploding onto the big screen in an adrenaline-fuelled epic adventure.'

GOUGHIE: 'To celebrate, talkSPORT are giving away an iPad and a whole host of *Expandable* goods in our ultimate action legends competition. Listen to Goldstein and Jacobs this week for your chance to win with *The Expandables Two*.'

And this is Micky Quinn and Mark Saggers handing out the prizes . . .

SAGGERS: 'Congratulations Duncan, you've won a thirty-two inch HD television and a home cinema. How about that!

QUINNY: 'And Cheyenne, you're not going away empty-handed . . . No sorry, you *are* going away empty-handed . . .'

This is Drive . . .

ADRIAN DURHAM: 'This is your tie-break question. In centimetres, what is the combined height of Nikola Zigic and Aaron Lennon? That's in *centimetres*. James, give me a figure.'

CALLER: 'Three thousand six hundred?'

(No wonder Zigic is good in the air.)

Micky Quinn's in the quizmaster's chair ...

QUINNY: 'Name one of the two colours that make up red or white – the national flag of Peru.'
CALLER: 'Can you repeat that, please?'
QUINNY: 'Oh, I'm confusing myself. It says name one of the two colours that make up the national flag of Peru. Red ... or white?'

(Ooh, it's a toughie ...)

***This was a question to a caller on Andy and Jason's* Weekend Sports Breakfast ...**

CUNDY: 'What was the approximate attendance of the crowd that day? Ninety-eight, eighty-six, or one hundred and two thousand?'
CALLER: 'What was that first one again?'
CUNDY: 'Was it ninety-eight thousand, eighty-six thousand, or one hundred and two thousand?'
CALLER: 'It was, I think, forty-two thousand?'

(Not quite grasped the concept of multiple choice, have you pal?)

OOH MY GOULD! (Bobby's Best Bits)

The 'Gouldfather' played and managed at the top for nearly 50 years and now brings the same level of energy and enthusiasm to Andy Goldstein's *Sports Bar* as he did to the dressing room and the dug-out. Looking as fit today as in his playing days, if Bob does have a slight weakness it's for remembering names. And pronouncing them . . .

The former Wimbledon manager and* Sports Bar *regular, with everything we need to know about Nigerian striker Yakubu . . .

'Yakuba? Well, his season's been start, stop, stop, go, stop, go from last season for Everton with the amount of injuries. He's got to start outing himself about and hopefully he can set himself alight this afternoon.'

(Thanks, Bob. We'll have the extinguisher standing by just in case . . .)

Co-commentating on the Dutch . . .

'Look at the shape – there's four men and two wide players either side, with Dick Van Dyke . . .'

With a revelation about Fabio Capello ...

'I still think Rooney is immature and he's not playing well at the moment. To put him in the side, the manager would expose himself.'

Bobby has a question ...

'With Liverpool struggling as they are, what do you think they'll need to put together in the January buying shop window?'

ALL IN THE WORST POSSIBLE TASTE

Tucked away in this selection are the clips you'll *never* hear again on talkSPORT. Aired once, then consigned to the audio skip of history. Until now . . .

Our man on Merseyside, Graham Beecroft, goes a bit Alan Partridge . . .

'Quite a few girls that go to university, pretty girls that I've seen that go to university, end up with pints of ale in their hands – and if there's anything less feminine than that, I don't know what is . . . apart from perhaps facial hair.'

Alan Brazil with an odd request . . .

'So this morning we wanted to know which song sums up your club's semen – sorry, *season*!'

Presenter Jon Gaunt making friends with newsreader Faye Carruthers . . .

GAUNT: 'I like synchronised swimming but they're all so ugly aren't they! Have you noticed that? Sychronised swimmers – why are they so damn ugly?'

FAYE: 'I used to be a synchronised swimmer.'

***A caller to* Fisherman's Blues ...**

'On the Monday before the competition, I was down there fishing with my friends Neil and Tom, and my rod's actually froze to the ground with icicles. It's quite a bizarre picture if you want to have a look at it – you're friends with me on facebook, have a little look and see the picture of these icicles hanging from my butt rings.'

(No, you're all right, mate ...)

Newsreader Peter Stewart ...

'The Bank of England have c**t interest rates ...'

TV columnist Garry Bushell discussing a showbiz legend on* Breakfast *with Alan Brazil and Mike Parry ...

GARRY: 'I feel a bit of fraud today.'
ALAN: 'Why?'
GARRY: 'Because I wasn't watching any TV last night – I was at the filming of the BAFTA tribute for Bob Monkhouse over at the BBC.'
MIKE: 'Bet that was a bit of fun?'
GARRY: 'Oh, there were some really nice contributions from some great people, including some of the best of the younger comics around now, like Jimmy Carr, Jack Dee and Steve Coogan. And the clips were absolutely sensational – they had all of his greatest one-liners, his acting roles, nostalgia by the bucket load. I mean you forget he was in things like *Carry On Sergeant*.'

MIKE: 'Well Garry, many people forget that he was one of the greatest stand-up comedians you've ever seen. I saw him years ago when I was a reporter in Chester and at the time we only knew him as the host of *The Golden Shot*.'

ALAN: 'I tell you what, he can do a blue version as well which is meant to be fantastic.'

GARRY: 'Oh yes, you can get those on DVD probably now. This tribute show goes out the weekend after next on BBC One. And you're right – you're left in no doubt that Monkhouse was a giant.'

ALAN: 'Garry, what about Bob's health now?'

GARRY: 'Er . . . he died at Christmas.'

MIKE: 'I think Mr Brazil was erm, just . . . just looking a little bit back there rather than forward...'

ALAN: 'I see. I heard two different versions of it, to be honest. Two different versions I was told.'

(Makes you wonder who was putting around the version that Bob was still alive? Think the great man would have seen the funny side of that one . . .)

AND FINALLY . . .

We could pretend otherwise, but these are the clips that didn't really fit anywhere else. It doesn't make them any less enjoyable!

Newsreader Liz Saul proving she's not quite the football expert we imagined . . .

'David Beckham will be officially presented as an LA Galaxy player tomorrow night; he and Posh leave Britain for America this afternoon. Becks is following in the footsteps of some of sport's biggest names, such as Joanne Croff, Franz Berkinborger and Gyorgy Best.'

Sports newsreader Elliott Cook – and if you're going to get one Fulham defender's name wrong, it's probably best it's not this one . . .

'Fulham face Danish side Ardense at Craven Cottage knowing a win would guarantee progression. Defender John Arser Riise says . . .'

***Drive** presenter Darren Gough didn't quite get the idea for that afternoon's* **'Listeners' Poll'** *...*

ADRIAN: 'The poll is a bit of reference to the F1 season and Cheltenham as well – it's simply this – horses or cars? Could be horse racing versus F1 or simply as a mode of transport – do you prefer horses or cars? What are you going for, Goughie?'

GOUGHIE: 'Motorbike.'

Sports newsreader Katie Murrells ...

'With the series already won, James Anderson has been arrested by England for the third Test against the West Indies ...'

talkSPORT overnight presenter Joe Holland with his thoughts on Posh Spice ...

'The funny thing is just how much Victoria Beckham seems to be loathed – I can't understand it. Apparently at a recent performance, she had fruit and vegetables thrown at her, poor girl. And they can be lethal. I remember there was recently a phase of a hooligan throwing vegetables out of a speeding car, and he caused no end of damage. I think he actually murdered someone with a turnip – was it a turnip? Or a carrot ... thrown at very, very high speeds.'

And he didn't leave it there . . .

'I was once told if you drop a pea off the top of the Empire State Building that it could cause death. Nasty business. It shouldn't be laughed at – some poor celebrity having vegetables thrown at them. Rotten tomatoes, you can just about excuse, I suppose. Eggs – eggs maybe. But the trouble with eggs is, what if they hit the celebrity on the temple sharp end up, so to speak? Because I was once told an experiment was done with an egg where it was dropped from a helicopter, it landed sharpest end down and it didn't crack – so presumably there must be a tremendous force there.'

Toby Gillies with football news . . .

'Leeds 'keeper Paddy Kenny has apologised to QPR owner Tony Fernandes after sending mocking messages. The former arse stopper sent the texts . . .'

(Pleased to hear he's given up the arse stopping, whatever that is . . .)

Newsreader Jake Robson . . .

'Silvio Berlusconi has been sentenced to seven years in prison. Italy's former prime minister has also been banned from holidaying.'

(So, no fortnight in Barbados for good behaviour, then?)

They've had some incredible guests on* Breakfast *over the years . . .

'Coming up, the youngest British female ever, Bonita Norris.'

(Doubt if she was much of a talker.)

Andrew McKenna with FA Cup fixture news . . .

'The first TV games for the fifth round have been confirmed – Arsenal or Middlesbrough against Arsenal will be on Saturday 28th at 5.15.'

(We fancy Arsenal in that one.)

Time now for the Newsreader of the Year Awards – and the winner of the 'Somehow Managing Not to Laugh' category was Robyn Schoenhofer . . .

'Opponents claim there was a widespread fraud. The winner was never in doubt says one of the election observers, Tiny Cox . . .'

Graham Beecroft with news for Evertonians . . .

'Chairman Bill Kenwright says that Roberto Martinez is going to be a man.'

Golf correspondent Bob Bubka lands an exclusive . . .

BOB: 'I'm going to say hello to John Paramore, we're talking live on talkSPORT. The course in good shape, John?'

JOHN PARAMORE: 'Fantastic.'

BOB: 'Fantastic. There he is, Head of Rules for the Ryder Cup, John Paramore, he told *you* on talkSPORT.'

(Hardly Frost/Nixon, was it?)

Exciting news from Derek Thompson on* Breakfast *. . .

'Guys, today at Wolverhampton it's Family Fun Day. They've got the Red Devils parachute team flying in, they've also got Spongebob – and Squarepants is there!'

(Spongebob and Squarepants. Quite a turn out.)

Newsreader Zora Suleman . . .

'Gordon Elvis has won the European Elvis Championships in Birmingham ahead of what would've been the King's 78th birthday. The Championship takes place every year in the Midlands – which is now in its tenth year.'

(Funny, thought the Midlands was older than that . . .)

Graham Beecroft with an important score update …

'Okay, we're just hearing it's Mansfield one Northampton nil in the play-off semi-final … sorry, Mansfield nil Northampton one, Mansfield nil Northampton one – Day getting the goal after forty minutes played. Northampton nil Mansfield one … I beg your pardon, let me get it right, Northampton nil Mansfield one in that play-off which is going on today. So it's Mansfield nil Northampton … sorry, it's Northampton nil, Mansfield one, let me get it absolutely right.'

(Any the wiser?)

And here he is again …

'I'm at Goodison Park at Sunday for the Everton game for the early kick-off – full commentary on talkSPORT, so don't forget to miss that one.'

(We were quite looking forward to it.)

Jack Bannister with news of Alastair Cook's dismissal …

'Cook had to suffer the dreaded finger – up it went.'

Keith Arthur on a missed media opportunity . . .

'I was actually involved several years ago with a budding TV channel . . . it was going to be during the day – six hours of angling shown twice and during the night – six hours of porn.'

(What a great combo – natural bedfellows.)

The Mirror's Darren Lewis on the Breakfast show . . .

'It must be bad for the West Ham fans to be chanting: "We want somebody in who is nowhere near proven as you say."'

(Not much of a chant, is it?)

Time for the travel now, with Alex Gale . . .

'The Portsmouth Road is closed in both directions due to a pretty big pothole in the road – it's around six foot wide and six foot deep. That's not really a pothole, is it . . . ?'

(More a meteor strike, Alex . . .)

Here's talkSPORT's Belgian football correspondent Rudi Nuyens on our show with his trademark sign-off . . .

PAUL: 'Good to talk to you Rudi, thanks very much.'
RUDI: 'Ah, no thanks at all.'

Here's the outspoken Adrian Durham with a bold claim ...

'I think that a cyclist will never win the Tour de France.'

The Moose getting to the heart of the Cesc Fabregas conundrum ...

'He'll go from being a big fish in a small pond at Arsenal, to being a small pond in a huge fish at Barcelona.'

(Thanks for that.)

Elliott Cook with the Sports News – and it sounds like Ramires has picked up a nasty injury ...

'Chelsea midfielder Ramires has been ruled out of tomorrow's game with Genk.'

(Is that like gout?)

Here's Dave Stanford with the travel news ...

'In Cambridgeshire, the A47 is closed in both directions – a lorry carrying potatoes has caught fire. So, plenty of baked potatoes!'

(Yeah, never mind the driver, Dave, think of the jacket spuds!)

Cricket correspondent Jack Bannister, with news of Ravi Bopara's favourite player . . .

> 'Sachin Tendulkar is Bopara's absolute hero. He's got pictures of Tendulkar batting and doing everything, in his bedroom and all round the house.'

(Like what? Hoovering?)

Time now for Ronnie Irani's thought for the day . . .

> 'There's nothing more satisfying than an ex-professional cricketer growing grass.'

(Sounds strangely profound, but probably isn't.)